I Heard Xavier Cry

A Decision Made with Love

I Heard Xavier Cry

A Decision Made with Love

By

Jude Emmanuel

Tahiti Press

Copyright © 2016 by Jude Emmanuel

All rights reserved

ISBN: 0692591508
ISBN 13: 9780692591505

This book or parts thereof may not be reproduced in any form, stored in

A retrieval system, or transmitted in any form by any means-

Electronic, mechanical, photocopy, recording, or otherwise without

Prior written permission of the author, except as provided by United States

Of America Copyright Law.

Published in the United States by

Tahiti Press

Scriptures taken from the Holy Bible, New International Version ®,

NIV®. Copyright © 1973, 1978, 1984 by Biblica, Inc. ™ use by

Permission of Zondervan. All rights reserved worldwide.

1. IBESR: Agency overseeing Domestic and international adoption in Ha

2. Hague Convention: International agreement to safeguard children in Intercountry adoption

DEDICATION

To the one my heart loves; my faithful and intimate friend. Your worth cannot be measured. You have proven to be a woman of grace, unparalleled strength and integrity. You inspire me daily. Thank you for your understanding and unbridled devotion to the spiritual vision. Know this, "Those who hope in the Lord will renew their strength; they will soar on wings like eagles; they will run and not grow weary; they will walk and not be faint." (**Isaiah 40:31**). Through you, I have received favor from the Lord. It would have been impossible to travel this journey without your love. You have been gifted with one of the most compassionate hearts ever to walk this earth.

You are beautiful

CONTENTS

DEDICATION

FOREWORD

INTRODUCTION   vii

THE ADVENTURE BEGINS   1

GRACE'S PROLOGUE   17

XAVIER IS BORN   24

TRIP TO HAITI   39

AN OMINOUS DECISION   78

CAPRICIOUS TRUST   87

KINDRED SPIRITS   98

RETURN TRIP TO HAITI   106

SHIFTING ATMOSPHERE   149

DIVIDED LOYALTY   157

MISSION DEFEATED   167

FILLING UP   179

THE AWKWARD SPACES   179

ALSO BY JUDE EMMANUEL

FOREWORD

ROMANS 8:28: "And we know that in all things, God works for the good of those who love Him, who have been called according to his purpose.

So the journey has come to this. It has inspired a novel birthed out of love.

For who has loved, without suffering any pain.

And who has not grieved, without first loving.

True love lies in the heart bleeding these inks. It has wings and

has traveled many places.

So fly on my friend, fly on.

Don't ever allow the evil of this world to clip your wings.

-- R.G. Lambert, Church of God, Brooklyn, New York--

INTRODUCTION

"We loved with a love that was more than Love."
Edgar Allan Poe

Out of an adoption journey, awakened an epiphany. The abstruse human heart, repeatedly the target of spiteful greed and reproach, will in due season discover its hidden flaws. Has a couple's caring nature taken for granted? Is the noble heart misguided by its own virtue? You be the judge, as Jude and Grace chronicle the details of a sordid and most unlikely tale of greed and deception. Married for over a decade, they would embark on a heartbreaking journey, which threatened to deprive their divine union of its innocence. They would soon discover, deceit indeed, can spring from the unlikeliest of places. This novel, inspired by a true-life story, recounts Jude and Grace's journey into darkness. A call to love had turned their dream into a nightmare.

THE ADVENTURE BEGINS

I remember that day as though it were yesterday. The streets were submerged with debris, as piles of dust, rained down as though from Heaven. The ground had opened, waiting to bury the dead. It was January 12, 2010. A 7.0 seismic earthquake had devastated Haiti. The destruction was vast, causing unimaginable devastation to the beautiful Caribbean Island. More than one hundred thousand dead they estimated, but I am sure it was more; it is always more. That night, the horrific catastrophe had hit home. The news rattled my mind with the unpredictability of an enemy's ambush. My whole body went into shock. I remember thinking about the children. Many of them running through the streets, trying to seek shelter amidst the rubble. The impact of the tragic earthquake, broadcast on television, sent a chilling shockwave throughout the world. The hearts of many, inconsolable, as they watched in agony. The destruction had overwhelmed the small island. That evening, I was so distraught by the calamity; I felt a drenching slug in my stomach. My chest began to burn with distress, as if it had been stabbed with flaming arrows. Disheartening--that's all I could call it. Holding my wife, Grace, embracing her as she bitterly wept. Her hands pressing tightly against her face, she could not hide her tears. "Jude!" She cried out, "What a horrible thing." Watching the broadcast on CNN in anguish, we felt hopeless. Haiti was *home*. Our people had experienced a terrible misfortune. "The children, oh my God, the children," Grace let slip. Her chest, jerked out with every gasp of torment breathed out, echoing what had been on my mind. Haiti was already home to a large orphan population even before the earthquake. Its streets would now be flooded with neglected souls. So many children would now be left without a home.

Grace and I began to worry about our family back home. When we finally were able to get in contact with them, hearing their voices brought us relief. Most of them had survived the horror. However, the exhilaration was short-lived. We would later find out, other family members were reported missing. The sting of misery had not escaped our family after all.

I Heard Xavier Cry

Some of our missing loved ones we would soon learn had met their end. The menace of the dark evening troubled me deeply. My heart ached with sorrow. How could God allow such devastation to take place? An overwhelming sense of compassion began to consume me. Rooted in it, was an awful lot of guilt, and a stream of self-indignation. It had been a while since I had deserted the homeland. It was now a foreign land to me. Haiti had raised me from birth and nurtured my soul. Its people were dark like me, but I had forgotten them. My Haiti, my beautiful Haiti and its children had suffered a terrible blow. They had already endured so much. But yet again, my Haitian people were reeling under the wind of another great misfortune. Tragedy had besieged the souls of Haiti's children, the little ones. It was cruel and unjust.

I had not traveled back home since leaving as a child. The torment of guilt was destroying me inside. Images after images of abandoned children permeating the television screen, further ignited a smoldering heap of an unfulfilled longing within me. What I had reasoned for a long time to be God's plan for my life was impatiently waiting to burst forth. I did not immediately share these anxious thoughts with my wife, Grace. Nevertheless, I began to wonder whether she was being confronted by the same restless thoughts. Grace and I had been together for more than a decade. We did not yet have any children. We mourned through an unexpected and painful miscarriage. Our love had covered the wound. We were always joyful in hope, trusting God's will to prevail. At times, we weren't quite sure what the Spirit was trying to tell us. The Holy Spirit, the Good Book said, would guide us. It had carried many to their rightful place of destiny. Hence, our faith rested in God's will, wherever it chose to lead us.

The long-lasting delay in having children, seldom frustrated our spirits. Thought it had done its best in trying to shame us, the longing cries of a hollow womb could not do away with our love.

"Don't you want kids?" Grace would say to me, having asked so many times before. She had practically memorized the answer. It had always been the same.

"Of course I do," I would say to her, wiping her cheeks after every midnight sobbing in the bathroom.

Surely I did; yet, my coronation of fatherhood was not going to be held hostage by a barren womb. To Grace, this was crazy talk, especially coming from her husband.

"I married a strange man," she would often say to me.

I Heard Xavier Cry

"Surely, you did," I would answer, always reminding her, my love would last until my last breath. We had come to appreciate the unpredictability of life. However, it wasn't always that way.

One has to adapt to whatever lot the Good Lord has assigned you in life, my mother used to say. Her words had come back to life. They were so vivid that day, a day unlike any other. When the doctor had called. I had a terrible feeling about what he was going to say. He had bad news, he told us. We had lost our baby. What does a man then say to his wife. Was it even possible for the flesh of her flesh to comfort her? When he, as well, thirsted for relief. Although the doctor's words had pierced deeply, I turned to the faith that led me to Grace. Our plight reminded me of the biblical tale of a good man, Elkanah was his name. He had two wives; one had children, while the one he truly loved did not have any. God had closed her womb. "Am I not worth more than ten sons?" Elkanah said to his barren wife. Though he tried, he was unable to comfort her pain. There had been times when I dared to wonder, whether these Scriptures had been written just so my heart could breathe. The words from the pages had suddenly come alive. They were like pellets of rain, hidden behind a dark cloud. They had breathed new life into our hearts. The words had always turned hard-luck into good, so we prayed. "You'll see, baby," I reassured Grace, without a shred of doubt the words would once again restore life into her womb.

Yet, it was almost impossible the Good Book said, for a man to console his woman, when her womb mourned in silence. The unfruitful womb, just like the grave it said, is never satisfied. There was something else I read, which was even more intriguing to me. God had purposely closed the wombs of so many virtuous women. Why had he done so? I pondered. Jacob, undoubtedly, must have known this. He is another man, the Good Book said, had no answers for God's mysterious deed. For when Rachel, his wife, complained about not being able to have children, he said to her, "Am I in the place of God?" A lot of men would have chosen to sacrifice a limb, rather than carry the burden of childlessness. That was not the struggle with my spirit. Though I was still grieving after the one God had taken away from us, who knows? Perhaps, it might have been what changed me. It had unchained my thoughts. Why toil over whether it is a boy, or a girl, when your precious joy can be taken away in the blink of an eye. It wasn't resentment, I told Grace. I refused to give up my soul for something we had no power over. If He did it before, God could do it again. But only if He wanted to. And if He didn't, who were we to accuse Him of betrayal. For who can open, what God has tied up?

Though we were still grief-stricken over the one we lost, our hearts ached to give more. This was how Grace and I lived. Our hearts were God's gifts to the world. Yet, He had taken away the fruit of our womb. We mourned through the pain on our own. It was not something we wanted to share with the world. It is often said, despair rejoices in the company it keeps. We declined to send out any invitation to our mourning feast. "Sometimes, those who mourn with you do so at your own peril," Grace would say to me.

After our miscarriage, we tried to move on, as far away from the bittersweet pain. We were young enough, we thought. We had plenty of time. Besides, time could heal all wounds, some would argue. So we waited, patiently. Though the passage of time had somewhat freed the sting from our memory, it was unwilling to gratify the womb. Years went by, no baby came. We then wished that time had the power to bring back the dead. Zaire, our lost son, could then be brought back to life. He would have been a prince you know, a prince amongst men. But, It wasn't God's will. "When are you going to have a baby?" people would ask. As if a baby came out of a book or by magic. They must have felt sorry for us, I supposed. It didn't bother us as much as those who thought we had been cursed. God had not blessed us with children, many whispered, because we were hiding a secret sin. How foolish! I thought. Whatever sin Grace and I might have committed must have been beyond forgiveness. If the tongue cuts like a blade, as it has been said, those doing the cutting were from our own house. Our house of worship that is. Surely, God had not forsaken us. For goodness sake, it's a good thing the Almighty had opened our eyes to those Scriptures. We forgave their ignorant talks. It was like hearing from fleeting shadows, or shaded lamps. And even if we were under God's wrath, who committed the unpardonable sin? Was it me? Was it Grace? Or was it passed down from generational sins? We were considered punished by God. Yet, many hearts, darker than ours, had been blessed with children. Some, had even neglected the fruit of their own labor. When we would hear horrific stories of abandoned children, our hearts would sink. "Why Lord? *Why*?" I would lament in the midst of our own suffering.

Then, came the night of January 12. The gloomy evening from hell. A burning desire had exploded within us, waiting to go up in flames. So started the adventure. For beginning that night, our lives would never be the same. Grace and I had our eyes glued to

I Heard Xavier Cry

the television screen, watching the unfolding event with great purpose at heart. Bodies of dying children laid waste on the ground. What would be the fate of those who had survived, with no one to care for them? We both lay in bed in utter dismay. The resonant voice of the television anchor was the only sound filling the room. Nonetheless, Grace and I were somehow communicating. Though our lips were not moving, our spirits were connecting. We would glance at each other every so often, with a raised eyebrow, or a chagrin frown. At one point, we locked our hands together and both let out a long anxious breath. What had been hidden inside of us had climbed out like the sun after a rainstorm. The desperate cry of an orphan had reached its journey's end.

We had always heard the orphans' silent cries, even before losing our beloved Zaire. Grace and I wanted to build an orphanage back home. We had planned on doing so after the birth of our son. But, it wasn't to be. Zaire had come out of the womb lifeless. And so, we waited. Once we had our own children, then, we would adopt. It was better this way, someone told us. So we continued the wait. Still, the longing to adopt grew even greater within us. It was as if we had been pruned like a tree branch. And now, we were even more eager to bear fruit. Wherever God had now chosen to lead us, we were ready to follow. And if it meant we needed to adopt, we were more than willing to fulfill our purpose. To us, children without parents were like scattered seeds, out-of-the-way of the gardener. They yearned for someone else to nurture them. We didn't need any more convincing, after what our eyes had seen. It was already written in our hearts and deeply embedded in our souls. We had waited long enough. A world filled with orphan children was beckoning us, singing to our hearts like a church choir's plea for mercy. If not us, then *who*? "Here we are Lord, send us," the thoughts prowled inside my head. Come to think of it, they had always been there.

Like the day when we came across this little boy while shopping at a local thrift store. It was a couple of weeks after Zaire drew his last breath. As soon as we entered the store, the boy started to stare at us. He appeared to be around ten years old. After picking out a few items to put in our cart, we noticed he was following us. He trailed us for so long, we finally turned to see if he needed our help. It looked as though he was creeping to come to us. He kept turning his head, looking to see if anyone was behind him. As he got closer, his face bright as the sun, and his lips, seemingly in a rush to speak.

"Are you guys house parents?" he asked.

I Heard Xavier Cry

Grace and I looked at each other with inquisitive smiles. We stood there—speechless—not knowing how to answer. What exactly was a house parent anyway, I thought? Thinking perhaps we did not hear him well, the little boy, determined to find out once again inquired.

"Are you? You look like house parents," he said.

We were yet again slow to answer. Grace and I had never heard of anyone being called house parents.

"Do you mean foster parents?" I asked.

"Yes! " He shouted with a smile, apparently relieved we had finally understood. I told him we weren't or at least not yet. His cheerful pose waned.

"You look like house parents," he muttered under his breath, as though disappointed.

We were both flattered by the boy's noble judgment of our character. People who took in neglected children in their homes were brave souls in our eyes. Then again, we did not know any foster parents. I wanted to know why the boy thought we were. Grace thought it was because he may have met other foster parents at the thrift store. There were other couples around, I told her; why didn't he ask them? As he was about to walk away, I asked him if he was in foster care. Before he could answer, "Steven!" a middle-aged blonde woman, storming out of the aisle yelled out, interrupting our chat.

"You cannot roam out of sight!" She said to him.

She looked upset, screaming at the little boy because he had wandered out of her view.

"Mom!" the little boy snapped back. Don't they look like house parents?" he said to the woman, anxiously waving his fingers towards Grace and me.

"Right, Mommy?" he frantically howled, hoping the blonde lady would approve of us, just as he had.

"If you say so, sweetie," she said to him. The blonde lady appeared somewhat embarrassed.

"This is my mommy," the little boy proudly said to us.

The blonde lady had three other children with her, two older girls, and a baby. As she perhaps realized, we were curiously staring at the two older girls.

"Ah!" she quickly chimed in.

She had detected the meddling thoughts behind our sneer.

"In case you're wondering, yes, these are my daughters," she said.

They were two beautiful black girls. We did not intentionally mean to stare. She told us, all of her children had been adopted; so was the little boy, Steven. He had been adopted from foster care since he was five.

The superficial glares did not bother her, the little boy's mother admitted.

"I love my children," she proudly declared.

She then told us something that reminded me of snow during the winter. As it rests on the ground, bright as sunlight, most admire it for a day or two, extolling its beauty. Yet, as soon as it gets in their way, they trample over its soft layer, crushing its ice crystals, turning the snowflakes into a murky swan.

"I know now why my son felt that way," the blonde lady confessed, carefully splitting glances between Grace and me.

"Tell me," I playfully said to her. Is it because we look like we hate children?"

She started to laugh, but then, her voice turned cold.

"No, hate is ugly, y'all look like a nice couple," she said.

She spoke with such conviction, I started to think perhaps our hearts had been deliberately put on display for the world to see.

"It's your demeanor, your ways," the blonde lady said to us.

"One can tell."

I knew where she was heading. We had heard it before.

"Tell what, that we have idiots written on our foreheads?" I replied with a chuckle.

"Oh no!" she said.

"It's love, it's written all over your face."

As open minded as we had been, the plague, which has driven so many away from adoption had traces of its ugly stereotypes in our hearts. I was just as guilty as everyone else for thinking the way I did. I had assumed they weren't a real family. Shame on me, I thought. They were a beautiful family, with a loving bond. Though I didn't offer any apologies for my rambling thoughts, I began to praise her in my mind. I looked from a distance when they were leaving, watching intently as the little boy, Steven and his two older sisters, lovingly embraced their mom. With each kiss, and every warm snuggle, they seemed to want to make up for all those moments they had been neglected by love. Their display of affection raided my senses like a cloud of burning incense. It had the fragrance of love poured out from Heaven. It did not matter that they had been the fruit of another woman's labor. If we had children, and we weren't able to care for them, I told Grace, "That's the kind of woman I would want to raise my kids." A surge of emotion had erupted in me, which has yet to go away. It was our first intimate glimpse of adoption. A seed of love had been implanted in us. We had waited long enough.

And so, the evening of January 12, 2010. The day we heard the children's footsteps. Not the loud steps, which had on occasions trampled our immaculate floor, but that of the children, who were fleeing from despair. Could God have been preparing us for such a time? Our hearts were like blossoming vines, ready for harvest. We had often heard, it takes a village to raise children. Grace and I made that village our home. "Her babies," as Grace loved to call them, had been raised by us as though they were ours. They were nieces and nephews, along with sons and daughters of friends. There were too many of them to count. We took care of them with selfless joy. Our home was like a castle to them. Our affection for these children were our testimony. Our love had enough zeal to cross the boundaries of our empty womb.

Though bursting a little with anxiety, we rushed to the cause with open hearts. With so many children likely to become orphans because of the earthquake, we desperately wanted to rescue one of the innocent souls. There were constant news reports of children being kidnapped. Others were being sold, or freely given away by poor families who were unable to care for them. The earthquake had created so much chaos, any semblance of child welfare policy had deteriorated into utter lawlessness. It was against this gloomy backdrop of uncertainty, Grace and I were called to the arena. Like two restless warriors, we felt compelled to engage the battlefield of hopelessness. It was time to fight the good fight, on behalf of the orphans. We could not remain idle and allow ourselves to be paralyzed by fear.

While we thought about adopting one of the young children in our family, these children weren't orphans. The call was not to them. It was to the deprived children. The ones shackled by rejection and neglect. The one at last, even the dust of the earth could not defeat.

GRACE'S PROLOGUE

Jude and I did not know how or where to begin. Ever so cautious, yet determined to follow our hearts, we were eager to travel the adventurous journey together. Things were awful in Haiti. The already dire living conditions of many had taken a turn for the worst. Haiti was like a war zone, undoubtedly not for the faint of heart. "Are you ready for the adventure, my love?" Jude asked. Of course I was. Nonetheless, we had never sailed across such an unfamiliar terrain. Where we excited? Certainly, but not without some trepidation. We contacted trusted friends and families in Haiti, letting them know of our plan to adopt. It was received with a mixed bag of emotions. While some were happy with our decision, others appeared to be skeptical. Their lack of enthusiasm was likely motivated by the volatile political climate in Haiti. They recounted horrible stories of adoptions gone badly. At the time, private adoption was not yet censored in Haiti. A system flawed with bribery and extortion was what we would be up against. Even with the forewarning of what was to come, we believed it was our divine assignment. We had replied favorably to the demands of destiny. It was now up to fate, to guide our steps in completing the journey.

Faithful calling had not delayed. It sprung forth from the most unexpected place one could have ever imagined. Niko, a trusted family friend, who had also been our wedding planner, called with exciting news. He had a newborn orphan baby boy in Haiti he wanted us to meet. The child lost both of his parents during the earthquake, he said. We didn't really know how to react, as it was a tragic story. Still, we were euphoric. It was not just a mere twist of fate; it had to be Heavenly orchestrated. The child's mother was Niko's cousin. We also thought of Niko as part of our family. It would be, indeed, an adoption made in Heaven. It was as though true destiny had disembarked from its sacred dwelling, wanting to steer our paths in this noble mission. Any traces of uncertainty were quickly disappearing. This was God's favor, clothing our hearts with joy. We had waited long enough.

I Heard Xavier Cry

Niko reassured us, the child was a healthy baby boy. Capricious, a cousin of the little boy's mother, found him nearly unconscious the night of the earthquake. Capricious was also Niko's first cousin. She and her husband, Salazar, were newlyweds. They were the ones caring for the little boy. Though they did not yet have any children, Capricious and her husband did not want to keep him. They were looking for other family members to help raise the little boy. But they couldn't find anyone willing to help. Niko thought Grace and I would be the perfect couple to adopt him.

That same day, Jude on one handset, while I anxiously listened on another, we initiated contact with Salazar and Capricious. The phone seemed to ring endlessly, as we waited for someone to answer. Finally, "Bonjour," the voice uttered at the other end of the line. It was Salazar. As Jude began the introductions, a piercing cry could be heard in the background. It sent a warm breeze down my belly. It was like the same gentle wind I felt when I discovered I was pregnant with Zaire. Jude and Salazar did most of the talking. Capricious sounded very timid on the phone. When Jude would try to engage her, she would mumble in one or two words syllables. "Yes, sir," or "no, sir," were the only words out of her mouth. The two men spoke for a long time. They were on the phone for what seemed like hours. "Moses," as we finally learned the baby boy's name, was now a month and a half. He was born a month before the earthquake. The couple found him near a ravine, close to his parents' home. His body was partially covered with dirt and surrounded by a sea of maggots. His parents were nowhere to be found. Moses was left all alone that terrible night. The same fate which took his parents from him had helped him hold on to his breath. The couple decided to name him Moses they said, because the little boy's ordeal reminded them of the biblical tale of a great man. "We have found you a young prince," Salazar declared with laughter. If their story sounded too much like a fairytale, we did not denounce the script.

Our Heavenly King had spoken. Any doubts about how the little boy had been discovered had quickly faded away. "This is prophetic; it is from the hands of the Lord," I said, as to the little boy's rescue from the jaws of death. Moses was like a plant, taken out of the ground. A flowering shrub, in search of rainwater, only to discover a river at its sight. In the place of skepticism, spiritual authenticity reigned. Moses' story was sure to become an extraordinary tale of love, hope, and restoration. It would be the sort of poetic justice displayed in Oscar worthy films. The stage had been set and the curtains uncovered. God had positioned us for a performance of a lifetime. Then again, the account of the little boy's young Journey was the genesis of an eerie and bittersweet nightmare.

With breathless anticipation, in what was to become our first opportunity to parent our very own child, we began to plan. We had to figure out how we were going to support the baby. Since we were going to be Moses' parents, we would now have to assume all financial responsibility. In the short time the couple had Moses, Salazar told us he and his wife had spent most of the money they had been saving to restore him back to health. It was incredibly generous of them, I thought; especially since they had just gotten married. "Our baby is in good hands," Jude would say to me. As we communicated more with the couple, we developed an excellent rapport with one another. Jude continually praised them for their extraordinary kindness.

One night, after Salazar had requested our email address, he sent us a picture of this awesome looking baby boy. The baby had a large afro, beautiful dark skin, and the loveliest brown eyes. He was a huge baby and strikingly well nourished. Salazar and

Capricious had apparently been taking good care of him. He had on a gorgeous yellow outfit, which Salazar said he purchased with money we had sent for Moses. We were so happy to see our new baby boy. Though adoption in so many ways may be a lot different than giving birth, the rush of excitement running through my body felt like the symptoms of a woman in labor. How could I know, you ask? It was through my pain. The ache which tormented my abdomen the night I woke up thinking I had delivered Zaire. With Moses, however, it was a sweet aching. A throbbing of a mother's love. My womb may have not nourished, nor delivered him, but my heart was aching to love him as though I did. This was our first time seeing our beautiful baby boy.

Since Moses did not own a birth certificate, Salazar suggested we register one, listing Jude and I as his birth parents. We didn't think it would work. We would then have to apply for him to immigrate to the U.S. as our biological child. It was too risky; they would lock us up in a cage, we told Salazar. We were instructed by U.S. Homeland Security, a DNA exam would most likely be required. They said we would need to have a blood examination done to see if we were Moses' birth parents. We were undoubtedly so tempted to jump into the lake of fire. But, it would have been like crossing the high seas in possession of stolen goods. Our minds would be filled with anguish, day after day, growing weary with fear, not knowing where we would land in the end. The mind can be skillfully deceptive, when it is motivated by selfish desires. Thus, we began to think of so many different ways for us to manipulate the facts. Our righteous Spirit, however, would not indulge. We were being led by a noble Spirit, which in no way would stray us toward a slippery path. We wanted to love, but not at the detriment of our dignity. Too much of a good thing can harm the soul. It's a good thing, the foretelling arm of destiny had intervened.

XAVIER IS BORN

Not wanting to complicate matters, Jude and I had Moses' birth parents' names registered on his birth certificate. Our attorney recommended we follow such course. He would be able to impose a *Conseil de Famille*. It would then allow us to establish a documented, personal relationship with Moses. His family would be required to appear in front of a judge, giving us permission to adopt Moses.

"Moses will be like one who comes from your womb," Salazar reassured me while speaking on the phone. He and I didn't talk much, but when we did, he made me feel as though we were bargain hunting for a child. We weren't shopping for a baby, as one shops for groceries, I told him. He didn't understand, but I am almost certain a lot of people didn't. We had waited on God, and once again, His timing was perfect. It was just like that song my mother would sing every Sunday afternoon; when I was growing up in Haiti. When she didn't know if we were going to have enough to eat. *"Bondye va voye kobo a vin lakay mwen*, (God will send the dove to my house.)" And God did. My mother would faithfully give Him praise. We never went hungry. Our table was always full. And so, deep within my soul, where God's Spirit lies, there was no doubt Moses would be our dove. He would be our bridge to love, in a way we could have never imagined.

Though "Moses," was a suitable name for the little boy, we wanted a new name for him. One, decorated with our own portrait of love. His family name would stay the same until the adoption would be finalized, but his first name, the intimate embodiment of how he would be known to the world, we wanted to make our own. Though he was not yet with us, like an inscribed necklace, we wanted to imprint him with our own stamp of entitlement.

"Xavier," I finally told Jude. "Xavier will be his name." It did not dawn on me right away, but deciding on this particular name was not just a coincidence. The more I thought about it, the more I began to realize it was fate's choice. Xavier was named after one of my favorite comic book heroes. Jude thought I had gone insane. "You've lost a few marbles," he said. Yet, there was more to the name than a mere wisp of imaginary bliss. Although the make-believe character had mind-reading abilities, the galactic aptitude was not the reason why he was so appealing to me. He had other powerful attributes, as well, which reminded me of Jude. He was soft-spoken, genteel, and affable, just like my husband. Much like Jude, the comic book hero also fought for the greater good of humanity. Jude did not appreciate me comparing him to an imaginary character. "It is a world of fantasy," he said. But in his heart, he knew the comparisons were true. Though Jude would never admit it, his discomfort with the character exposed a weakness in him. As though he was afraid to look at himself in the mirror, fearing he would discover his own flaws. "Why fight for a world, which does not appreciate you," my husband often jeered, ridiculing the character. Yet they did—they mirrored each other in a lot of ways—even in their thirst to study the human mind.

While Jude had also been a good judge of character, he as well had tasted the bitter scornfulness of the world. Though he, at times, had been bruised, he seldom struck back. No matter how hard he tried not to forgive, my husband's compassionate heart wouldn't let him. Forgiveness was like a thorn at his side. And so, he lived on with the invisible scars. He may have thought he had kept them well concealed; even so, I witnessed his struggles. I had seen my husband be an angel to a world, who, time and again, returned his love with contempt. It was as though the world wanted to condemn a man, whose sin was to love. He continued to love without complaint. His ways were wrought with pleasant and familiar aroma. I thought of the man who had been despised by mankind, and yet would willfully fall on a sword for me, a Scripture I once read came to mind. It said, "He was oppressed and afflicted, yet he did not open his mouth; led like a lamb to the slaughter, still, he did not open his mouth." The Scripture had not lied; all of it was true. Jude had turned into this obedient soul. The transformation started after his "coming to Jesus moment." It happened the night he and I met, he said. He could not put it into words, but he sensed that something was peeling away at all the darkness he felt inside. It was as if he had been hit by a beam of light. The beast within him had been transformed into a new creature. He was a new man. I dared not scorned his confession as empty words. I had seen the change; I was a witness.

Though we couldn't have predicted it, we were about to go through a storm. One, unlike any we had yet to face as husband and wife. Although the man with the good heart once said to me, "Baby, you are God's grace to my soul," the raging storm would threaten to devour both of our souls. Its wings would spring wide, hoping to carry us away with its ferocious winds. A storm was coming. We could feel it. It started with a soft breeze.

One day, we received a call from Niko late in the evening, while Jude and I were preparing to go to bed. Niko sounded awfully upset. His voice quivering in panic, he wanted to know if we had been sending money for Xavier. A woman who apparently was babysitting Xavier called Niko in a fit of rage, demanding we send money for Xavier to eat. Who was this woman? And what happened to Salazar and Capricious? There had to have been some sort of misunderstanding. It was both embarrassing and confusing to us. We had sent money for Xavier the night before. It felt as if we had been struck in the face with our own hands. That night, we tried endlessly to reach the couple, but we couldn't find them. Calls to their phones went unanswered, as if they were purposely avoiding us. The next morning, Salazar finally returned our calls. He could not offer any reasonable explanation for what had transpired. His usual, briskly tone, sounded more like a frightened swindler. He seemed so aloof, we didn't know what to make of his vague answers. "That woman shouldn't have called," was the best explanation he would offer. He insisted it was an honest mistake. Xavier had plenty to eat, he told us. He refused to tell us who the woman was that called. He would only disclose she lived in the house. "Trust me," he said, "I'll tell you later who she is." Salazar told us the woman did not know where he and Capricious had hidden Xavier's food supply. When asked why they didn't answer our calls, Salazar said they were at church. Jude and I did not press the issue any further. Later that same week, Salazar finally revealed the woman's identity. It was Capricious' sister, he told us. "Trust me, I' ll tell you later," he pleaded once again. He still couldn't fully explain why she had called.

Niko was like a middle- man between us and the couple. He, Capricious, and Xavier's birth mom were altogether first cousins. The strong family ties, notwithstanding, Jude made it clear to Niko, it would be best for us to work directly with the couple. There were sure to be a lot of muddled communication with Niko as a mediator. Besides, we wanted to keep things private. A bond of three always leaves one scorching in flames, a great woman once told me. Our plan was not to allow ourselves to fall into those dark clouds.

The burning coal had already touched our feet the night Niko called. It had Jude burning with anger. "I don't know if I should still trust him," Jude said, concerning Niko. It was just a hunch, he said, which made him question Niko's allegiance. Jude did not appreciate being interrogated, as though we were felons. "What if you're wrong?" I said to him. It didn't matter; the seed of distrust had already been sown. The way Niko spoke to him that night, Jude thought, showed a lack of respect. My husband had been shoved by the blast of air of an evil wind. "We have to scale the walls of truth," Jude often cautioned. We may have thought of Niko as a man of candor, then again, what is vile doesn't always come from the hearts of those with evil intent. I thought my husband was being too paranoid. He hated putting his trust in people. It was as if he was afraid every evil he saw in their hearts would one day bear fruit. Jude trusted Niko, but he knew Niko's loyalty was to Salazar and Capricious. After all, they were his relatives.

"In doing good, let not your left hand know what the right hand is doing," the Scripture said. I read it over and over again and made it our banner of integrity. Whenever we came to the aid of others, it was done without a trumpet blast. We didn't do things to be rewarded, nor for accolades. Jude warned Niko yet again—it is out of the thirst of a good deed, he told

I Heard Xavier Cry

him, we had chosen to adopt Xavier. Jude thought perhaps, even Niko had assumed we were desperate to have a child at all costs. "Why now? And why Haiti?" he told Niko. Our town in Philadelphia had plenty of foster children available for adoption. Niko didn't understand, just as he couldn't fathom why we had insisted on keeping the adoption private. At least, until we were close to the end, we told him. We could not let everyone in on our plan. Sounding very much like a charismatic preacher, Jude would say to me, "Listen, love," before he would start to preach. His voice, shivering, as though he secretly wanted to charm me.

"Do you know why, God favored Abel's offering over Cain's?" he would ask.

The answer was never foreign to me. He had expounded this sermon so many times. And yet,

"Tell me, love," I would answer.

He would then turn to me with a thoughtful gaze.

"Well, Cain presented a sacrifice with hidden motives, while Able offered one of goodwill."

The answer was always the same. As amusing a discourse it was, I always listened with a discerning ear. His sermon resonated like the rendering of a frantic television evangelist. His words, faithfully rang true. The man with the kind heart had spoken. At times, it looked as if my husband was preaching while standing in the middle of a train track, seemingly oblivious to the hurtling train fast approaching. Dark shadows obscured his vision, but I always covered him. He always did the same for me.

When we agreed to adopt Xavier, Niko told us both Salazar and his wife were unemployed. It didn't come as a surprise to us. A lot of people in Haiti were struggling to get by without a job. I often wondered how the couple had been able to care for Xavier. They had enough to eat and a place to sleep. Nonetheless, they were far from being well-off according to Salazar. They were living with Salazar's parents. Fortunately, his parents had enough financial means to help support them. Salazar and his wife would sometimes travel to the Dominican Republic to sell goods. It wasn't always profitable Salazar admitted, but it helped them put food on the table. Commerce was the way of life for many in Haiti. To some, that is all they had to sustain themselves. That's how they were able to provide for their entire household. Selling of goods was like a sacred ritual. It was *God* to some, and the breath of life to others. My grandfather once called it, "The engine of all saints."

I Heard Xavier Cry

Salazar was also a choir director. He would sometimes get paid for his piano lessons. It didn't pay much; so it was not enough. While the couple had also traveled to other Caribbean islands for commerce, Salazar contended they didn't make as much money doing business in these other markets. It was honorable of them to take in Xavier, which, without a doubt, disturbed their travel. However, Salazar told us even before they took in Xavier, he and Capricious had decided to pursue other business ventures. Hence, while not incredibly wealthy, Salazar had found different ways to provide for his wife. Jude and I truly admired them for having the courage to help care for Xavier. When we found out Capricious had been taking Xavier to church, it was like hearing the sound of sweet melody in the morning. We were excited to learn that our baby boy was in the hands of God-fearing people. While going to church didn't necessarily turn the couple into saints, we rejoiced, nonetheless. It was indeed more than a twist of fate. The hands of God were at work. Like a sheep, we were relying on our instinct, following a harvest, which looked ripe of promises. We had decided to follow where our hearts were leading us. Then again, slowly but surely, we were being led along a path filled with iron thorns.

Although we marveled at the way the couple had been caring for Xavier, a few things began to trouble us. What we dreaded the most, the very thing Jude had warned against, had reared its horrid crown. We learned from my aunt, Clara, Capricious started to complain about us not sending enough money. Aunt Clara and Niko were good friends. She had heard it from Niko, she said. Jude was once again furious. He didn't have to say a word. The tightening of the skin on his forehead told me everything I needed to hear. If this was Niko's ingenious way of relating the message, he certainly succeeded. He knew Aunt Clara would tell us. She had been a strong advocate of the adoption. Jude thought it was a shrewd move on Niko's part. Niko was acting like an assailant. "What a big-time hypocrite," Jude called him. He thought we were being ambushed. Telling Aunt Clara was like stabbing us with a dagger behind our backs. Niko knew, full well, the couple's grumbling would upset her. She was not happy to hear about Capricious' complaint. This was why my husband had been so cautious. Jude hated pretense. His voice was filled with so much rage. He sounded like a lion on a hunt. "Why didn't Niko talk to us?" he asked, with a seething anger. We had pleaded with Niko to come to us, if he felt there were any issues to go over. I was trying my best to damp the raging fire out of my husband. He had warned me. The deceitful and undercutting ways of Salazar and Capricious started to build resentment in him.

After the incident, a wall began to develop inside my husband. I could see it in his eyes. It was as if he were fortifying a tower for a battle he had long waited for. Jude always shared his deepest thoughts. This time, however, he was reluctant to tell me why his anger had risen to such a depth. Then again, he didn't have to say anything. As his wife, I knew what was troubling my husband. We were joined at the hip. Jude could handle all sorts of spiteful reproach, but he didn't like to be deceived. He had always been a reflective and thoughtful man. Yet now, his cynicism had become almost like a sickness. It seemed to be picking at his heart, bit by bit. Although the way Niko had acted made me uncomfortable, he didn't appear to have done so out of spite. Jude thought differently. "It feels like a bad omen," he said. A sign of more terrible things to come. Even if Niko had acted callously, I thought, it might have been because he hadn't fully come to grips with our motivation for wanting to adopt Xavier. It was a decision made with love, not out of recklessness. I was not going to put up a fight with my husband. What if I had assumed incorrectly.

Our adventure was quickly turning into an endless journey. But, as time passed, Jude was no longer drenched with anger. He cautioned for us to keep a close eye on both Niko and the couple. Jude didn't like to hold on to anger. It made him feel as though he were locked in a cage. "I am doing it for the kid," he said. He had decided not to even say anything to Niko. As for Salazar and Capricious, telling them off didn't even seem to matter.

"If they are fishing, they will get trapped in their own net," Jude conceded.

"Besides," he added, "Would God let it happen?"

Putting aside their indiscretion, we increased Xavier's monthly allowance. We figured the couple might have been uncomfortable asking us for more money. Perhaps, what we had been sending was not enough. In spite of everything, neither Salazar, nor his wife was working.

While we wrestled with our thoughts, trying to figure out why the couple had not confided in us, I kept praying for Xavier's sake. Thankfully, things seemed to settle down. Capricious was awfully cheerful when we agreed to add to Xavier's allowance. She even admitted, the additional cash was more than adequate. "Oh my God, you will be blessed," she said.

I Heard Xavier Cry

However, what had we done? The couple had somehow stirred our noble hearts of our own free will. The floodgates of greed, then began to loosen its chained fences. Not a week would go by after we had sent money for Xavier, without Salazar calling me with a cunning soliloquy. He had a peculiar way of asking for money, which often made me furious. He would preface his speech, telling us, "Today is Sunday." At first, we couldn't figure out what he meant. Then, we soon realized it was his way of asking for more money. When we would remind him, we had already sent money for Xavier, he would stay silent on the phone. We hardly scuffled with him, however, over his crafty demands. I am not sure why we never did. Yet, for the first time since we decided to adopt Xavier, I felt as though we weren't doing enough. I pressed my husband to do more. It was an anxious push, as in the worried thrust of a woman in labor pain.

Jude so desperately wanted to protect me against the ensnaring net of Salazar and Capricious. However, he had not traveled to Haiti in over twenty years. Things had changed for the worst. Life wasn't the same. Everything was a lot more expensive. Raising a child in Haiti was like growing a garden in infertile soil. Only God could predict how the crop would turn out. Capricious might have thought the money we were sending was more than enough, but Xavier was now *our* baby. If it meant allowing his caretakers a little freedom to splurge, so be it, I told my husband. Salazar was the one helping to coordinate some of the adoption paperwork. We always sent him travel money, but he was also taking time away from his personal affairs. I went to war with my husband on behalf of our baby. Though Jude admitted defeat, there was still a seed of doubt creeping in.

Xavier was still very young. We wanted him to know us. I longed to see him and cling to him with loving hands. Thankfully, I would not have to wait long. We received a call from our attorney in Haiti. Jude and I would have to appear in court, to pledge before the law, our intent to adopt our son. Thank Goodness! I was beyond ecstatic. A long awaited trip to Haiti was approaching, but more importantly, I was going to see my baby.

TRIP TO HAITI

My excitement was much more temperate. Grace and I were preparing to travel to Haiti, to see Xavier; yet my heart was bursting with discomfort. I struggled to avoid any strife with Salazar and Capricious. Grace had persuaded me to put a muzzle over my mouth. I began to notice some disturbing trends with the couple. They were not so easy to dismiss. As soon as we started sending them more money, things started to change. The roles had shifted. The couple began to display a different image of themselves. Often acting with an air of entitlement. They acted so arrogantly at times, one would have thought they were mobsters, waiting for the perfect opportunity to strike. Capricious was no longer the shy personality on the phone. She was now bold and full of haughtiness. It's a good thing she and her husband mostly communicated with me. Though they didn't know it, I had intentionally planned it that way. It was best for Grace to stay in the shadows. The couple had lost my trust.

The couple's attitude had become so outlandish. Whenever we would send money, they no longer called to confirm they had received our transfer. "That is so trivial," Grace would bark at me for complaining. I knew I hadn't suddenly lost my wits. Unless we called, we would not hear from them until it was time to send money again. We would usually get a call the day before we normally wire the funds. They would call and put Xavier on the phone. Beyond a doubt, I told Grace, it was a ruse to soften my mood. And yet, it always worked. There would always be this melancholic chill, spiraling through my bones. It happened every time I would hear Xavier's voice. Capricious would then get on the phone, reminding me about Xavier's ferocious appetite. On other occasions, if the money arrived a day late, she would start to complain as though she wanted to start a riot. "You have a son to raise," Capricious would say to me. She acted as though she were a loan shark, and I was her game. Taking care of Xavier was now done as a favor to us. Things had changed, but I kept quiet. I did not tell Grace. A child's life hung in the balance.

I Heard Xavier Cry

My silence was necessary; the stakes were too high for us to change course on a whim.

A couple of weeks before our trip, we learned through Niko, Capricious was expecting. The couple had not told us about the pregnancy. It might have explained their recent changes in behavior. I felt a great sense of relief. All of my worries were perhaps unwarranted. The stress of the pregnancy could have been too overwhelming. Add Xavier to the mix, it would unquestionably be even harder to cope. I couldn't fathom why they didn't tell us, but I figured they would eventually let us know. A week before traveling to Haiti, Salazar called to share the awesome news. He was so excited. He was finally about to become a dad. However, the good news did not come without some compromise to our adoption. After the tragic earthquake had taken Xavier's parents, he did not have any legal guardians. We had arranged through the courts to have Salazar and Capricious serve as his legal guardians. But, Capriccios' name was the only one listed on the document. Salazar wasn't able to make it to court with her that day, Capricious told us. She was now unable to travel. She wasn't feeling well. Who then, would be going to court with us? With only a few days left before our trip, we needed to find a quick fix.

With his wife pregnant, Salazar suggested we appoint somebody else as Xavier's guardian. Capricious would not be able to travel all the time, and he needed to be with her, he said. Fortunately, Marie-Loraine, one of capricious' sisters, we were told agreed to be registered as Xavier's legal guardian. Salazar and Capricious would still nonetheless be the ones taking care of Xavier. Marie-Lorraine was a young woman in her early twenties, according to Salazar. She wasn't married and did not have any children. She would be free to attend the many immigration appointments before the adoption would be finalized. It was not supposed to be this complicated; yet we were so thrilled when the young woman offered to help. She would now be our guardian angel in court.

The couple lived in a remote province, about fifty miles north of the capital of Port- au- Prince. The roads were in such a poor condition, we sent roundtrip airfare for everyone to travel. We did not want Xavier to suffer through the four hours it would have taken by bus. Strangely, the fare was terribly expensive for a flight lasting no more than half an hour. Still, we were willing to do anything, to accommodate our baby.

October 30th, 2010, Grace and I traveled to Haiti in the middle of a devastating cholera outbreak. An additional 200,000 souls would ultimately succumb to another tragedy, nearly ten months after the earthquake. I remember praying after hearing about the outbreak, asking God, if our lives, Haitian peoples' lives that is, did not matter to Him. So many of those lives lost were innocent children. My mind then wandered to a Scripture that says, "Precious in the sight of the Lord is the death of his faithful servant." Still, my conscience wrestled with God.

"Is that of benefit to their grieving families? Is this how one comforts their moms and dads?" I asked.

The Scripture was merely words, I thought, empty words to these inconsolable parents. I tried to keep the thoughts at bay, far away from my mind, but I couldn't. They kept coming. I couldn't control them. I better plead for forgiveness, I started to lament with tense breaths. Conversely, those "Moms" and "Dads" were weeping in despair, I cried out to God. Tears of bitterness were spilling down their sorrowful faces. I knew some of those faces, whose pain had shut their lips from uttering a word. I heard their tearful souls. Those parents were grieving as I had been. Who was I to even be thinking this way? My voice had been heard, and my grumbling thoughts answered. "For who has understood the mind of the Lord, as to instruct Him," another Scripture, in a flash, rammed through my head. The Spirit was talking to me, crushing the pride of my own will. I was so afraid by now; my thoughts were running scared. Then, as if a ghost had whispered into my ear, I was reminded that even Grace and I were being molded like clay. God's truth has a strange way of vindicating itself. There we were, enjoying a beautiful and happy life in Philadelphia. But now, we were about to leave the comfort of our beautiful home to travel in the midst of a cholera outbreak for a child we did not even know.

There were plenty of other children we could have chosen to adopt around the world. Yet, we couldn't alter the course even if we wanted to. The cries of the child trapped underneath the rubble had grown so loud, not even the mountains, nor the endless seas, could halt the sobs from leaping into our hearts. Fate wanted the dance to be with Xavier and him only. Right before we were getting ready to travel to Haiti, a colleague at work had asked why were we going back home. When she found out it was because of an adoption, "Jude!" she gasped, "I didn't know, I didn't know," she said. She did part-time work for a foster care agency. They were trying to find a good home for two young children, who had recently become available for adoption. The children were four-year-old twins. Although they were in a temporary placement, she wasn't sure if they could wait for us to get the required training and other clearances.

"There are a lot of neglected children here," she said, trying to convince me Haiti was not a safe place.

"It's home to me," I told her.

I thought a lot about those children after she recounted the horrible event that brought them into foster care. Then again, God had other plans.

We were strongly discouraged by a few family members living in the U.S., not to travel to Haiti. Along with the Cholera epidemic, there had also been rumors of kidnappings of the diaspora—Haitians living abroad. Nonetheless, there was a persistent nudge delving into me, pushing me to go the way fate had intended. During our flight, Grace appeared to be extremely nervous. "What the heck are we doing?" she asked. Though she might have asked rhetorically, I had no answers. We both then started to laugh, as tears of joy dripped down our faces. It had already taken us too long to finally see our son. We so desperately wanted to see him. We were drowning in our own wave of anticipation.

Finally, after more than twenty years of voluntary exile, I was home. Grace had gone back many times to see her family, but I had not. There were no words to justify my shameful neglect; no excuse to dress up my guilt. An émigré! I shouldn't have been. As soon as we landed at the airport in Haiti, I was overwhelmed with unease. Though Grace didn't look as tense, my heart was jittery. I was going to be reunited with family members I had not seen in over decades. The burst of anxiety sent butterflies down my stomach. The scorching sun, I remember thinking it was the sun that made me feel so jittery. It had welcomed me home with scorn and covered my head with a cloak of guilt. "Oh Haiti," I wept, "forgive me." I felt the reprisal of its forsaken love.

My cousin Mario picked us up at the airport. He and his wife were one of the few family members who knew about the adoption. As we drove to his house, it amazed me how much Haiti had changed. Mario highlighted how crippling the impact of the earthquake had been. There were many people still living in makeshift tents. Seeing the devastating effect of the earthquake on my *people* left me with a conflicting array of emotions. On one hand, I was distraught by how dreadful some of the streets looked, but I also felt a sense of pride. There was a compelling beauty and resiliency in the Haitian people. They held their heads up with dignity. As men and women of valor, they pressed on in the midst of the frail landscape. Splendor had not completely alienated the beautiful island. I immediately surrendered to its serenity. It was home.

Grace did not say much throughout the whole ride. She repeatedly gazed at the people walking the streets. I wondered what was going through her mind. Was she thinking about Xavier? With a deluge of gut-wrenching emotions confronting me, I had not thought much about him. A guilty conscience had unmasked a heavy heart. Xavier was the sole reason for my visit, after so many years of being away from home. I had not returned to visit since leaving as an adolescent. Yet, there I was, after more than twenty years away from the homeland. A foreign child to my family, had gotten me to move my feet, and return home in the midst of chaos.

"We here," my cousin Mario shouted in English. When we arrived at his house, we were immediately greeted by his wife, and his two beautiful children. Everyone was extremely accommodating. That same night, they delighted us with a welcoming patty. We were greeted by family members, whom I was meeting for the first time, and others I had not seen in decades. Many childhood friends also took part in the festivity. The food was awesome. We enjoyed black

mushrooms rice and beans, with avocados, and fried pork chops—the much celebrated "Haitian *Gryot*." As if we had not had enough, they also served us fried sweet plantains and grilled conch, doused in tomato sauce. Last of all, we were indulged with Papaya and cherry juices, bolstering further our insatiable appetite. While we weren't unaccustomed to eating Haitian cuisine at home, the local food was prepared with an added splash of aromatic piquancy.

No one questioned my motivation in finally deciding to return home. There was not a single remark from anyone. Yet, I'm sure everyone knew my reason for coming. These clandestine undertakings do not remain secretive for too long. While we very much appreciated the courtesy, keeping the adoption private started to weigh heavily on our minds. No matter how forcefully my guilt-ridden conscience wanted to hold me captive, the rules of engagement needed to prevail. We weren't going to suddenly renege on our plan. It was for a noble purpose. We hoped that everyone would understand. Nevertheless, could they? At the family gathering, as jokes were being exchanged, one of my uncles made a vague remark about a friend looking nothing like his father, suggesting he was adopted. One could have heard a pin drop in the room, had it not been for the music playing in the background. There was utter silence, as my cousin's wife shoved my uncle with a nervous nudge on the back. "Be quiet," she said to him. Everyone was trying their best not to look my way. They bowed their heads to the floor, as though they were in prayer. Grace and I were not at all offended by his innocuous jesting. We had traveled over fifteen hundred miles, to fulfill a dream we could have chosen to satisfy years ago. And, pursue it under the comfort of our own backyard. There was no discomfort in us wanting to adopt. The awkward feeling, which slowly started to build up, was because of the unknown child we espoused to raise as our own. Surely, my family had not, nor would they ever understand. Soon after the party, Grace and I retired to bed. We were so exhausted, but also euphoric in anticipation of meeting our son the following day.

We woke up early the next morning to the intoning cries of roosters, signaling the dawn of a new day. They had prepared us a splendid breakfast, fit for a king and queen. We had grilled salmon, avocado cornmeal, with poached plantains, and freshly squeezed orange and pomegranate juice. The meal looked extremely appetizing, but this time, we were not that hungry. I ate a small portion, while Grace only had a cup of coffee. We had planned on meeting Salazar at Grace's aunt's home. We would be spending a few nights at her house. It was an ideal place to meet, since her home wasn't too far away from the airport.

As it was coming close to the time of our rendezvous, my cousin Mario agreed to drop us off. We arrived at Grace's aunt's house early in the afternoon and waited impatiently for Salazar to come. Grace's aunt had recently traveled to the U.S.; so she and I had met. We had never discussed our adoption plans with her, but like everyone else, she eventually found out. However, she never said anything. Shortly after our arrival, while chatting upstairs in the balcony, Grace and I noticed a car pulling in the driveway. A lady was holding a baby in the back seat. We speedily ran down the steps, sprinting all the way out to the driveway. As we began to approach the car, a tall, dark-skinned man, sporting a nineteen eighties afro, and what could best be described as his "Sunday's best" exited the passenger side of the vehicle. While we had never seen Salazar, not even through pictures, we immediately knew it was him. As Grace made her way towards him, the lady holding the baby boy also exited the vehicle.

"Capricious!" I shouted, staring at her belly.

"It's me," she replied, appearing a little nervous.

I Heard Xavier Cry

Salazar, who meanwhile was greeting Grace, swiftly turned to me and started to explain why Capriccios had showed up instead of her sister. Marie-Lorraine couldn't make the trip he said, because of a family crisis back home. Therefore, Capricious decided to come. Grace and I were so lost in the moment, neither of us thought of asking how Marie-Lorraine's absence would affect our court date. We were so happy to finally meet Xavier.

Capricious appeared much younger than I anticipated. She was a well-dressed, and attractive young woman, most likely in her early twenties. She never shared how old she was, and I never inquired. We all made our way inside, after the apparent taxicab left. As soon as we had made it inside the house, Capricious handed Xavier to us. Grace and I reached to grab him almost simultaneously. Grace took a hold of him and stubbornly tried to plant kisses on his cheek. Xavier repeatedly attempted to pull away. He eventually relented, smiling uncontrollably, as he surrendered to her smothering kisses. Xavier was a handsome kid, with a gorgeous smile. He couldn't stop laughing, while Grace playfully stroked his huge stomach. He had the most stunning brown eyes I had ever seen. He looked so much like Salazar and Capricious, if I didn't know better, I would have guessed he was their son.

While Grace continued her amusing tête-à-tête with Xavier, he turned to look at me, reacting to my shameless peck on his forehead. He appeared confused, trading hasty stares between Grace and me. Our flattering gazes perhaps, caused him to look at us in astonishment, or conceivably it was because we kept speaking to him in English. Although he might not have understood our spoken words, the look on his face spoke loudly. He knew we loved him. He continued to stare at me, while resting his head on Grace's shoulder. I then took him from her, telling Grace It was time for me to hold my son. I lifted him up in the air like a tribal king, proclaiming the glorious arrival of a first-born prince. This was our baby boy, our long-awaited son. We held on to him for what seemed like an eternity, forgetting the couple was in the room. Xavier's charismatic smile had us molded to him like wallpaper paste. We eventually apologized to the couple for our apparent lack of decorum.

After spending time with Xavier, we sat down to talk with the couple for some time. They seemed somewhat standoffish. Talking to them was like talking to a wall. They did not say much. Grace noticed how they constantly looked at each other in disgust, while we were holding Xavier. Since it was our first time seeing our son, we had hoped they would have understood, but apparently they didn't. We would not realize how upset they were until much later. They went to Niko with a tsunami of complaints, telling him how callously I had treated them. If our only sin had been spending too much time with Xavier, then we were as guilty as they judged us to be. However, it would become apparent, behind their conviction, hid an ensnaring campaign, which would help cover up their own sins.

It was not until we sat down to talk with the couple, I would suddenly grasp the gravity of Marie-Loraine's absence. After being told, Capricious would not be able to make the trip, she showed up without warning. Unless she or Salazar could legally show they had parental rights, they wouldn't be able to give consent in court. It started to get hot, scorching hot. I was now burning with rage. Though the room we were in was already warm, fluid was now leaking out of my body. It was pouring out of me like a violent heave of an ocean. Madness wanted to take over, but I held it in. No wonder they were acting so strangely. Salazar seemed very shrewd; yet sometimes he acted as though he were thoughtless. He wasn't that foolish. His reckless attitude was deliberate. When asked why he did not tell us Marie-Loraine would not be able to travel, Salazar deflected the question in Machiavellian arrogance.

"No big deal," he said — Capricious and I will sign."

He knew it couldn't be done. The law would not allow it.

"What does this mean for us?" Grace asked.

She was beyond angry. We were only going to be in Haiti for a few more days. We would have to reschedule our court date.

Then, the mysterious phone call came. The one about Marie-Loraine. All of a sudden, Salazar felt the urge to tell us the real reason why she was not able to come. He had received a call on his cell phone while talking to us. It was the voodoo priest, Salazar told us, asking for money. Marie-Loraine was apparently being held hostage by this witchcraft priest, and he was demanding a large ransom for her release. The extraordinary tale tormented my spirit. I was skeptical of the couple's true intentions.

"It's not a lot of money," Salazar mumbled, suggesting for us to pay the ransom.

When we told him we wouldn't, he insisted the ransom was only a few thousand U.S. dollars. I wondered what in the world made him think we were going to lay down like fools and pay it.

"No way," I told him, Grace and I would never agree to such demand.

Our stay in Haiti was not going to be long. There was not enough time to transfer custody back to the couple. When our attorney suggested other options, Salazar claimed Xavier's birth certificate, along with the other documents were with Marie Loraine. Grace and I traveled to Haiti, filled with joy, but our jubilation didn't last long. Although we were overjoyed to be with Xavier, we had to cancel our court date. What a wasted opportunity, I thought. Grace and I were going to return home with fainted hearts. I wanted to end everything; God had anointed the wrong candidates for the task.

While we would have liked for Xavier to spend the night with us, we decided against it. We were too overwhelmed with resentment and greatly concerned with the couple's lack of candor. So many things were sifting through our minds. Though Xavier was like a young bird without a nest, Grace and I had one built for him. That night, however, I wondered whether our efforts were in vain. Was it our punishment for loving an orphan? We fell in love with him the first time we laid eyes on his beautiful smile. But for some reason, my love started to taste bitter. Xavier left with the couple that evening. They were staying with Capricious' uncle, who lived only a few miles away. Throughout the night, Xavier prowled over my thoughts like a thief in the night. He was all I could think about.

The following day, we were awakened by a call on my mobile phone early in the morning. It was Salazar, sounding overly dismayed and upset. He called to inquire about a smartphone we had promised to get him.

"Why so early in the morning?" I said to him.

The clock was just turning seven. It should not have been such a surprise. This was how Salazar functioned. The most trivial of things always seemed to matter more, especially when they were of benefit to him. I had carried a large suitcase filled with diapers, baby clothing, as well as a host of other items. Clearly disappointed he could not locate the phone after going through the suitcase,

"All I see is a bunch of baby clothes," he said.

It was not what an already disenchanted heart wanted to hear. We simply forgot to give him the phone, which was still in our luggage. I thought it was rather selfish and arrogant, the way he referred to Xavier's clothes. His brazen disrespect bothered me. He acted as if he were receiving a bribe. Since we were still going to see our attorney later that morning, we agreed to meet thereafter at Capriccios' uncle's place. We could not wait to see Xavier again.

As we were on our way to see Xavier, after a brief meeting with our attorney, Salazar called and insisted on us meeting him a few blocks away from the house. He claimed to have been involved in a squabble with the people they were staying with. My cousin Mario, who was our chauffeur, was not at all pleased to hear this. He was visibly annoyed. He was a man of few words; yet, the look on his face spoke to me as if it were shelling out words. When asked if he thought Salazar was not telling the truth, Mario humbly answered with a shrug of the shoulder. He seemed not to want to affirm, nor refute the obvious. Whatever he was thinking, he did not want to disclose. There was no need to further examine his thoughts, as he repeatedly kept shaking his head. Grace did not utter much neither. If my quiet laughter wanted to betray any bottled-up cynicism, I did not want to arouse it. My expression might have appeared to be calm, yet I could feel the hot fumes coming out of my nostrils. Grace and I had been there before. Salazar's story sounded like a shadowy plot. As we approached the intersection of our place of rendezvous, Salazar was standing there, alone. He had promised to bring Xavier along. When asked why Xavier was not with him, he looked around before answering, acting as though he was afraid he would be caught in a lie.

"Xavier doesn't feel well," he whispered under his breath.

He had to leave him behind. And we couldn't come to the house to see him. There were a lot of things going on, which he could not explain. Our conversation was brief. He infuriated me so much, I didn't even want to give him the phone, but I reluctantly handed it to him. I reminded him that Grace and I would be leaving the following day. We wanted to see Xavier one last time before we leave, but it was not going to happen. Grace was livid. She tried to hide her anger, pressing her teeth tightly against her lips. Her face turned red, covering her radiant beauty. "What the heck," she muttered in disbelief.

Driving back home, there was such a conspicuous silence in the car. Not even the radio was turned on. When someone finally spoke, it was my cousin Mario at last, affirming his frustration. "I don't trust that guy," he grunted with a restrained tongue. He then turned to look at me and said, "Jude, be careful."

Though I had not shared with him our increasing trepidation regarding the adoption, I didn't have to. Driving home, he recounted a depressing story about a pastor and his wife. The couple lived in Atlanta, Georgia, he told us. They wanted to adopt the pastor's two-year-old niece, who lived in Haiti. Everything had gone well, he explained, until the night before they were scheduled to travel with the little girl. Masked gunmen entered the home in the middle of the night and kidnapped the little girl. The kidnappers held her for ransom. Luckily, her captors were later apprehended. After a thorough investigation, it was discovered, the pastor's sister had hired the abductors. She had her own daughter kidnapped, Mario told us.

"Why?" He said with a slight chuckle, relentlessly tapping the wheel, with the might of a lion warning his cub.

"Greed!" Mario scoffed in disgust.

The pastor had been sending his sister close to four hundred dollars every month to help care for her daughter. With her little girl gone, she wouldn't be getting the same amount of cash. Her daughter's promising future did not matter. As Mario was telling the story, a Scripture, cautiously guarded in my heart, spurted out like an arrow out of my lips.

"The love of money is indeed the root of all evil," I said to him.

Jude Emmanuel

It is the affection for greed, my pastor would preach, that drives people's evil motives. It is not wealth itself—for everyone loves money. That woman had allowed greed to overpower sound judgment.

"So, be careful Jude," Mario forewarned once again.

He was like a big brother to me. Mario was my closest cousin and a good friend. He was somewhat reclusive, but when he spoke, words of wisdom soared from within like a prophet's cautioning tongue. He was in his late thirties, yet wise beyond his years. I had listened to him attentively and heeded his advice. Nonetheless, considering my own ways, I thought, even if Salazar and Capricious were in a quest to hunt, there was no way I would allow them to devour us as prey.

When we finally made it back to the house, Grace and I were emotionally exhausted. We knew the adoption would have its moments of hills and valleys. Yet, after each climb, our hearts grew weaker. We ceaselessly worried; the next hike could be our last. The process, we anticipated would be a tough journey, but loads of worries with Xavier's caretakers, we did not expect. We kept hope, nonetheless. Our attorney was incredibly supportive. He was more like a friend. During our meeting with him earlier that morning, we told him how worried we were with the couples' recent odd behavior. He tried his best to encourage us not to lose hope. However, he admitted to having his own doubt. "Be sure, these are people you can trust," he said. We were so lucky to have retained him as our attorney. He seemed empathetic and was exceptionally skillful at managing adoption proceedings. When we started the process of researching attorneys, he was not our first choice. We had contacted several other lawyers, but they were ridiculously expensive. Moreover, they did not appear to be well versed on how to finalize the adoption with U.S. immigration. Grace and I had done our own research and gained a lot of insight on the many legal nuances of international adoption. Particularly in Haiti, where the process was like walking through a maze.

We were well prepared to assess whether or not an attorney was up to the task. As private adoption, with nominal legalities, was still permissible in Haiti at the time, there was no need to apply through an adoption agency. An immigration attorney would not have been able to navigate the initial domestic adoption. A lot was required before applying for an Adoptee visa to the U.S. Thus, it was important for us to retain an attorney who was well-informed. As we quickly learned, there had been many cases of which children were adopted in Haiti, but could not travel because of immigration problems. Grace and I went to great lengths, not to allow such misfortune to be our fate. Even though we did not want to solicit the help of adoption agencies, we did contact more than a few in conducting our research. Most of them had temporarily suspended all international adoptions from Haiti. These were not adoption agencies unfamiliar with Haiti international adoption. These agencies had offices with more than a few personnel in Haiti. Yet, they were scrambling to reassess their Haiti adoption program after the earthquake. These agencies were justified in their apprehension, as Haiti would soon experience a shift in its adoption procedure that would threaten to foil our plan to adopt Xavier.

Nevertheless, a series of events had emerged, which reassured our belief, a hand greater than ours had been steering the wheels of the adoption. As a child growing up in Haiti, I had befriended a boy who lived in our neighborhood. We became very close friends. We used to go everywhere together. At dinner time, it was not uncommon for us to share the same plate. After leaving Haiti, we lost contact. He and I had not spoken in over twenty years. Grace and I were so astonished when we learned that this childhood friend was now a high-ranking administrator at "IBEsR." It was the government agency overseeing adoptions in

I Heard Xavier Cry

Haiti. This was an eerie twist of fate. After spending so much time not speaking to one another, it felt awkward for me to all of a sudden reach out to him. It was beyond a doubt, what we needed to help our cause, but I was reluctant to call. It would make me feel as though I was a con artist. This was not who I was, I thought. But, a strange thing happened. As luck would have it, then again, it was more than luck, I did not have to call him. Fate had stirred his heart. He found out about our adoption plan through my cousin Mario and wanted to help.

It was about two weeks after Grace and I decided to adopt Xavier. We were still in the process of trying to find a good attorney. We couldn't believe he had placed a long distance call, reaching out to help an old friend, who had forgotten about him. What's more, he had experienced a tragic loss during the earthquake. His wife had succumbed to the tragic event. When he and I finally spoke, I was speechless. It was as if nothing had changed. He displayed such grace and humility. This was truly the fabric of character of a great man, I told Grace. No wonder he and I had been close friends at one time. He had gone over the list of things we needed and even offered to personally oversee our case. He had done enough. We were beyond grateful. He then recommended a top of the line attorney, Robert J. Belizaire, who also worked at the agency. The path could not have been laid out any smoother for us. Grace was so excited. "Stuff like this don't just happen," she proclaimed with joy.

As soon as we contacted Belizaire, there wasn't any doubt that he would be our attorney. He was exceptionally knowledgeable, and yet also a little bit arrogant. Though he did not appear to lack any self-confidence, underneath the swagger, however, was a thoughtful and family man. He was sympathetic to our mission. He even offered his services pro bono, but we declined the offer. It didn't feel right for us not to pay him. While he had the privilege of agency resources at his disposal, we wanted to honor his services appropriately. He, nevertheless, offered us a considerable discount. Belizaire even warned us about some of the drawbacks we could conceivably face, with us not using an agency. "Nothing I can't handle," he bragged. Touting his religious belief, Belizaire cautioned us not to pursue the adoption, unless we were certain it was what God wanted for us. It was a peculiar advice, I thought, especially out of the mouth of an attorney. Yet, he had a wealth of experience with adoption procedures. He shared some of the horror stories with us. He told us about countless adoption cases, in which parental rights had not been officially terminated. In many of these cases, he disclosed, the adoption was rescinded. Many adoption documents, as well, he added, had been falsified, only to be discovered later as fraudulent by U.S. immigration.

Belizaire wanted to know all of the details relating to Xavier's birth parents. If it couldn't be proven that they were deceased, further motions would have to be filed in court. When we told him the account of how Xavier had been discovered after the earthquake, there was a confounding silence on the phone. I could hear his shallow breath, so I knew he had heard me. After waiting patiently for him to answer, there was a humming sound filtering through his hoarse voice. He then asked,

"Are you sure about doing this?"

I knew what he was thinking; it had also crossed our minds.

"Absolutely," I answered.

Belizaire jokingly retorted, since we already agreed to pay him, he would gladly take our money. Although we would not meet face to face until my travel to Haiti, our attorney and client relationship had grown into a friendship. He hated it when I would tell him he sounded more like a preacher.

Thereafter, Belizaire yet again, expressed his concern about the adoption, following our meeting. He suggested we take time to think over our decision. It was our fourth night in Haiti, but it felt like we had been there much longer. While we were having a wonderful time with family, Grace and I were beginning to get tired. It was mostly mental fatigue. We called Salazar and Capricious to see if Xavier felt any better, but they did not answer. This was our last night in Haiti; we wanted to see him before leaving. It was getting late in the evening, so we decided to pay one last visit to a friend. The outing turned out to be a lot more fun than anticipated. Friends gathered to throw us a farewell party. This was the remedy needed to lift up our spirits. One last night of enjoyment with family, friends, and delightful cuisine. We had "Fritay," another famous Haitian dish—made of mostly deep fried pork and other fritters. However, what gives this appetizer soul is the legendary spicy Haitian vinaigrette it is typically served with. The "Pikliz," as it is famously called by the locals.

The ambiance had been so uplifting, it prompted me to shout out, "Lakay se lakay"—home sweet home. The gag brought so much laughter into the room. Everyone looked on with amusing grins as I gobbled down the food. We all were having a fun time, recollecting old tales of childhood moments, when all of a sudden, the music stopped. My cousin Mario handed me his mobile phone with a puzzled look on his face.

"You have a phone call," he said.

He could not make out who it was. The caller sounded agitated. *Who possibly could it be?* I thought. I had not given Mario's number to anyone.

"Who is this?" I asked, as my mind began to race in panic.

"Niko? What's going on?" I shouted in utter disbelief.

He sounded extremely upset. He then told me how Salazar and Capricious had frantically called him, complaining they were stranded and could not return home. They told him I had not given them enough money to travel. There was more, Niko continued. Their visit had been so disastrous the couple told him; they felt as though they had been treated like rootless dogs.

I impatiently heeded every word in astonishment. It felt as though a jolt of electricity had entered through my veins. It would have been unjust of my righteous Spirit, to douse the raging edict of fire burning within me. This was more unsettling than a mystery flick.

Much like a horror movie, it was turning into a nightmarish mission in Haiti.

"Hell no," I said to Niko, feeling my chest burning with wrath.

"Lies, a bunch of freaking lies," I yelled out to him.

"Relax, Jude," Mario quickly interjected, before I could finish.

Everyone in the room had their eyes on me. The couple's silly antics had become far too familiar. The humble heart of clay, being led by the Spirit, was quickly turning into timber.

"That's it! No more, I'm done," I told Niko.

Mario, then, told everyone to leave the room. I told them they didn't have to. What would be the purpose in hiding what was looking, more and more, like an extortion plot.

"We have had enough," I once again said to Niko.

There were few words out of Niko thereafter. He was only relating a message, he said. We had sent money for Salazar to purchase roundtrip tickets, I told him. Furthermore, why were they calling him? Salazar had woken us up early that morning, begging for the smartphone; yet somehow could not remember to tell us they had no money to return home. When we dropped off the phone in the afternoon, he yet again, failed to say anything.

"You know why," I said to Niko. "Because he's a con artist. And how did they get this number?" I curiously inquired.

Niko thought I was fussing too much over the matter.

"It's probably just a huge misunderstanding," he concluded.

How convenient, I thought. I was having a déjà vu moment. It had happened before, and Niko's response had been the same. "Just a misunderstanding," he alleged, the night Capricious' sister called. She had asked Niko to have us wire money so she could purchase food for Xavier. The couple was nowhere to be found that evening. They claimed they were at church. The way Niko spoke to me that night, one would have thought I was a deadbeat father, evading child support. This time, however, I wanted to make sure the arrow of criticism would crook back to the one holding the bow. Niko had engaged me in warfare. When he realized his armor was weak, he quickly retreated, making an impassioned plea for peace.

After speaking with Niko that late evening, my restless attempts in trying to contact the couple were useless. They weren't answering their phones, just as they did the night they claimed they were at church. I was curious to find out what their excuse would be this time around. The next morning, before boarding our flight, we tried once more to get in touch with the couple, to no avail. Needless to say, it was becoming very apparent something sinister was taking place. Regardless of how it was going to end, Grace and I vowed to remain peaceful. It was fate, undeniably. Fate had brought me home. It had carried me back to my roots. I couldn't wait to return to the foreign land—I now called *home*. Our spirit appeared to be weakening in defeat. "Where are you?" I said to my Lord. The Spirit seemed to have turned a deaf ear to me. The trail of our mission was leading us into what seemed like the deceitful stillness of a jungle, peacefully waiting to demolish its prey. We were obviously upset, yet not discouraged beyond hope. Faith would not allow it. It was about to restore our fading passion in a most peculiar way. How else could one explain the strange incident shadowing our spirit during our return flight to Philadelphia?

As soon as we boarded the plane, we noticed a man behind us with a baby in his arms. Soon after take-off, the baby began to cry relentlessly. The man then left his seat, pacing up and down the aisle, trying to get the baby to stop crying. She was a beautiful baby girl, we assumed was his daughter. The little girl continued to bellow out her honeycomb cry, like the sweet cry of a newborn just out of the womb. Back and forth, the man strolled along the aisle, until he abruptly rested next to our seats. Firmly holding on to the little girl, he started to sing to her. However, she did not show much interest in his harmonizing chant. The baby girl apparently had other plans. She began to struggle with the willpower of a bird in captivity. The man had endured more bodily harm than he could bear. He was being punched and kicked all over. He looked like a man in peril. Just before he turned to walk back to his seat, the little girl leaned ahead, grabbing Grace's shoulder. The man, looking exasperated, bowed down to the little girl's demand. He gently handed her over to Grace without uttering a word. Apparently exhausted, and in dire need of relief, he let out a loud breath before returning to his seat. Suddenly, the little girl's tears had come to an end. She looked my way and started to tug my shirt. Not a minute later, we turned back to see whether the man wanted her back, but he had fallen asleep.

The little girl spent most of the flight pulling at my shirt and playing with Grace's necklace. She refused to go to sleep. Grace had asked me to grab a bag next to the man's seat. It had baby food in it, so that's all she ate. She did not appear to be more than two years old. By the time the man had finally awakened, the little girl was now fast asleep in Grace's arms. As we approached the end of the flight, Grace handed the little girl back to the man. He then told us a story our ears could not fathom. Just as we suspected, the little girl was his daughter. She was adopted, he told us. His wife stayed back to nurse his mother-in-law, who was battling cancer. The little girl was also his niece. Her mom died during the earthquake. The man and his wife had already adopted the little girl even before his sister's tragic death. "We don't know her dad," he said. It was his first time traveling with his adopted baby girl. She was just about to turn two. The man then asked if we had any children. I didn't know what to say to him; neither did Grace, her chest rising with a tense jolt. She seemed lost in her own world, looking at the man with a blank stare. Was this some perverse prank? I pondered. Heaven would never allow me to be mocked in such a way, would it?

"No kids yet," I finally answered, as I thought about Xavier.

Grace did not say anything. Her eyes were brimming with tears.

"Really!" The young woman seated at the other end of the aisle chimed in.

"You guys were so good with the baby," she said.

My heart shivered, wanting to sink to the ground.

"You will make great parents one day," someone else nearby shouted.

"It's okay," I answered, feeling a soft quiver down my throat. "Whenever God decides."

I wanted the flight to end.

After we had landed, the man started to follow us, as we exited the aircraft. He said he wanted to thank Grace for helping him with his daughter. He had a look of disappointment on his face. After making our way through customs, the man continued to trail us. He called out to me and whispered almost out of pity,

"Have you thought about adoption?"

He started to bite into his lips, as though he had been too embarrassed to ask.

"We're trying," I said to him, with a heavy heart and a huge lump in my throat.

As we were leaving to go our separate ways, holding his daughter on one hand, he pressed on my shoulder with the other.

"I understand," he said,

"She's my only child."

Shortly after arriving home, I noticed several missed calls from Salazar on my cell phone. He was so predictable. His follies were often followed by gauzy speeches. I often couldn't decide whether they had been excuses to cover his track or the remorseful plea of a lying tongue. They had become the same to me. It was certain, the skillful craftsman had carefully forged another one of his sorry excuses. My body was still filled with so much rage. My bones were rigid, like iron. My entire body then became numb. I couldn't feel a thing. The Spirit had crushed me with my own anger. Though broken, my heart yearned to listen again. It didn't make any sense for me to be feeling this way after I had been so angry. Such a strange thing God had done. Perhaps, it was because of what had happened during our flight. I was, yet again, ready to forgive. Salazar was calling again, just as I started to think about Xavier. I thought a lot about him. I had seen my reflection in his eyes. They had captured my soul. His cheerful fragrance had traveled across the Caribbean waters with me. What was happening to me? I had wrath, a bustling anger inside of me before leaving Haiti. And yet, I sensed my iron-will being buried now that I was home. Something in me was trying to restore the hope of a broken dream.

"Baby," Grace called out to me with a loud cry. "My spirit feels so broken," she said.

I Heard Xavier Cry

What a strange thing God had done. We wanted to hold Xavier again.

The phone was ringing once again.

"Pick it up, hear what he has to say," Grace pleaded with me.

We couldn't wait to hear the craftsman's sob story.

"Jude, I am so sorry. I can explain," Salazar, sounding like a man cringing in fear, muttered as soon as I picked up.

"What in the world is going on?" I asked.

He went on to explain he had been too embarrassed to tell me the truth.

"Anh! The truth," I said to him, turning to Grace, who had an edgy look on her face.

Though Salazar told us he had purchased the airline tickets ahead of time, he had lied. He waited until they had gotten to the airport to buy the tickets. By that time, the price had already gone up. He was only able to get one-way fares. A friend had recommended buying the tickets the same day. The airline typically dropped the cost for same day travel purchases, the friend told him. Either the friend was misinformed or Salazar had crafted a lengthy speech. His explanation was tenuous at best, if not contemptibly dull. I didn't know what to make of his story.

"Why lie then?" I asked.

He couldn't answer.

"I am sorry, okay," he kept repeating, as though he had wished he didn't have to explain anything.

His hasty tone was begging me to let things go. I wanted so badly to tell him off and thought about doing worse to him. But then, the unimaginable happened. I could hear my mother's voice on her dying bed.

"Jude, my son," she said, looking straight into my soul with her tawny eyes.

"God has changed you; the Spirit has washed your tongue," my mother held on to my face with both hands. Grace sat beside me that day. My mother loved her. But Grace loved her even more. My mother knew it was because of Grace. God had used her to purge the demons out of her son.

I found myself being convicted by a greater Judge, for what I thought about doing to Salazar. It was as if I was the one on trial. Why had my heart become so weak, so forgiving? If we had been doomed by fate, if it had wanted to condemn us, we didn't put up any

I Heard Xavier Cry

defense. Its mighty hand had gotten us to forgive Salazar. Perhaps it was because of Xavier. Deep within, I wanted him to be ours. He would be the son I never had. The will of God was not done with us. Fate had positioned us in a collision course with love.

As for why he and Capricious told Niko we had treated them like dogs, Salazar quickly denied his involvement.

"It wasn't me," he said, blaming his wife for the incident.

Yet again, the skillful artist was at work, betraying his wife's trust for his own gain.

"I have a favor to ask," he then calmly muffled.

He wanted us to bail him out, begging me to pay for their return trip home.

"We have no money, and Xavier is getting cranky," he said.

As he was speaking, I heard Xavier crying in the background. My anger had completely withered away. It retreated like turbulent waters, abandoning the seashore. Because of Xavier, because of the orphan I wanted to be my son, I had agreed to Salazar's demand.

"I want this boy home," I said to Grace.

She told me not to worry.

"I won't let you ride this ship alone," she uttered with tears.

Her face told a different story. The fading hope of a jaded spirit was in her voice. Though Grace vowed to climb the mountain of love with me, I did not know how much more she was willing to swallow.

"I will ride with you for now," she said, after I had pressed her to tell me what was hidden in her heart.

My beautiful bride had gone through countless struggles with me.

"Jude," she said with weary breaths. "I'm starting to lose my will for this."

AN OMINOUS DECISION

Several weeks had passed after I had agreed to pay for Capricious and Salazar to return home with Xavier. During that time, we didn't really communicate much with the couple. There were still a lot to think about. Grace and I spent this period of respite, trying to reconnect. Not that we had pulled away from each other. We missed our intimate times together. We missed us. It felt as though we hadn't seen each other in months.

"We were a lot happier without all this mess," Grace grumbled.

How could that be? I thought. Yet she was dead-on. Things were different. Loving Xavier brought us a lot of joy, yet also a lot of grief. Our love wasn't the same. It wasn't any less than it had been. It just felt different.

Perhaps that's what happens when people have children, I said to Grace. It was a different kind of happy.

"Why are we doing this again?" Grace asked, scanning through some of the adoption documents.

I looked at her, puzzled, and somewhat afraid.

"Xavier, of course, darling," I answered, not sure where it was going to lead.

Was she going to tell me to put an end to the adoption? I wasn't ready to move on. She then flaunted her beautiful smile.

"Xavier, my baby," she said, taking a quick glance at his picture on her phone.

"This one, I like," she said, lifting her fingers off the screen to stare at the picture.

"I miss being with him," Grace let out softly.

"I think a lot about him as well," I told her.

We weren't ready to give up on him, not without a fight. Things had to change, however. Salazar and Capricious had totally lost our trust.

Like a dying tree, thirsting to sprout up, good news was about to delight our hearts. Nearly a month after returning from Haiti, we received a call from Niko

I Heard Xavier Cry

with a curious proposition. He suggested we have one of our family members take custody of Xavier until the adoption would be finalized. The man who once walked with integrity in my eyes, perhaps had heard my silent grumbling. Good for him, I thought. He had redeemed his integrity.

"Why didn't we think of that?" I said to Grace.

As it turned out, the good news had dimmed our spirits, just as quickly as it had renewed it. It was like receiving a sweet and sour treat all at once. Moving Xavier would offer the ultimate bliss. He would be with family, thus freeing us from the heavy hands of the couple. Besides, Haiti only had one airport accessible for international travel. It was far from where the couple lived.

"Let's move him," Grace maintained, beaming with excitement.

Once more, however, the wheels of destiny had intervened. Moving Xavier would have its own thorns. We weren't sure how our family would feel about him moving in. Would they understand? Many of them had young children close in age to Xavier. Would they resent us? The whispers behind the curtains had already begun, Aunt Clara told us. The chatter had family members prying into our affairs like bees after a honey jar.

"Where did they find this kid?" some wanted to know.

"Is he part of the family?" others inquired with acrimony.

After hearing this, I started to think, having Xavier stay with our family might not be such a good thing. I, once again, felt a fury of haziness within me. But this time, guilt threatened to boil over a heart already filled with uncertainty.

Sending Xavier to live with family would be like asking the queen's family to raise the love child of a king. He would be treated as a foreigner in his own household. A bastard child, some would even dare call him. I did not want to do it. It wouldn't be fair to sacrifice my son's dignity for our own comfort. I did not share these thoughts with Niko when he first called. I told him we needed to think about it. Fate, however, wouldn't even allow enough time to ponder over our decision. I was quickly swayed by the demoiselle in distress. It was as though she had read my mind from a distance. My cautious delay was her strength. For when Capricious heard about Niko's proposal, she balked at the idea, sobbing uncontrollably like a grieving mother.

"Oh my God! Xavier will be miserable," she pleaded with me.

"You know it, Jude—you know he will," Capricious implored, as she bitterly wept.

There was no need for her to speak another word. My veiled thoughts had already come out of her lips.

"Enough!" I said to her, in a fit of rage.

I wrestled with fury of hesitancy inside of me. Not because she had persuaded me against my will. She didn't have to. I was left without a choice. My heart was being ripped apart by both love and guilt. It chose love. Nonetheless, I had relented too easily without questioning Capricious' true motive. Grace and I agreed, Xavier would be better off staying with the couple. Yet, in doing so, we had unwittingly engraved the tombstone predestined to bury the adoption. I did not know it then, but that night, I handed Capricious the key to my house. She then had the freedom to do as she desired.

"Are we still following the will of God?" Grace asked, examining my thoughts.

"Of course, dear," I reassured her, not entirely convinced.

When it comes to the law of providence, there are neither right, nor wrong decisions. All things come to pass, as they are intended to. As I later attempted to undo what I finally realized might have been a critical blunder, I quickly discovered, the wind of inevitability had only been delayed. God was about to show us His wisdom, by turning our weakness into a strength.

Perhaps, it was the calm before the impending storm, but after allowing Xavier to remain with the couple, sunshine reigned in our house once again.

"Thank God! There is finally peace," Grace would sing each morning. Things were going so well between us and the couple, it felt as though my decision had been vindicated. I was now able to see the end of our adoption journey. It was, without a doubt, going to be a smooth paved road.

"The harvest is near," I would tell my beautiful bride.

Though peace and joy always rested at our door, this gladness of heart felt a lot different. We were preparing to receive a new child into our home. Beyond excited, we finally shared the good news with everyone.

As things started to settle down, it allowed us a chance to reflect on one of the biggest decisions of our married life. Though adoption may not be for everyone, and certainly not for the faint of heart, Grace

I Heard Xavier Cry

and I were more than willing to shoulder all of its burden. "How will you handle it?" Many in our family had asked. They wanted to know, could we really love a stranger's child. I didn't see it that way. God's wisdom had been transforming my mind. Grace and I would go to many funerals, and when we would get to the burial place, the tombstones would speak to me. Not in words or visions, otherwise Grace would think I was insane. But, there would be so many of them.

"Look!" I would say to Grace, "Each grave has its own story to tell."

Yet, no matter the size of their tombs, death had conquered them all. The poor, the wealthy, the famous, and even those without honor. We will all go down the pit one day, I would say to her.

"Our time here on earth is short," I told Grace. "We should live it with love, even if it is all we have to give."

One day, as we were about to bury another dead, we arrived at a crowded funeral home. There were at least three viewings taking place at the same time. Next door to our viewing room, there were loud cries, which overshadowed the grieving shouts weeping for our own dead. I went outside, wanting to get a closer look. Two young men were walking alongside this frail, older looking fellow. Each of the young men at his side, they were holding on tightly to his arms as though they were armor bearers. The older gentleman looked as though he had been sniffling a lot of tears. He had a bunch of balled-up tissues in his hands. His eyes looked as though they had been victims of many sleepless nights. He then sat on a bench outside of the viewing room, while the two lads gently slapped their hands on his back. They looked like two young warriors, eager to restore the strength of their master. The older gentleman peered my way, and saw that I was staring.

"Come here," he said.

As I got closer to him, one of the young men called out.

"Dad!"

But he wouldn't let him finish. He raised his right hand, as though he were a king, hushing the crowd.

"I'm talking," he said to the young fella.

I almost exploded with laughter. My father would have done the same thing.

"Did you know Samuel?" he asked.

As I was about to answer, he rushed to inquire yet again.

"You must have known my son Samuel," he said, in a proud voice.

I suddenly caught on; Samuel may be the lifeless body inside the casket.

"No, sir," I replied, all the while thinking, it was my punishment for snooping.

"Good kid, good kid," the man repeated.

By this time, he must have realized I had been grieving my own death, next door. But he didn't seem to care. He just wanted to talk. He went on to explain that Samuel was his youngest son. He was murdered while in a bar fight with friends. One single bullet in the back of his head did it, the man told me.

"What a horrible thing," I said to him.

There was nothing else to say to ease his pain. However, it was the words he had uttered as he was about to leave that haunted me for a long time.

"It is better to not have one at all than to have one and have God take it away," he said.

CAPRICIOUS TRUST

Though oceans and mountains separated us from Xavier, our hearts grew closer to him every day. We could not wait to see the day when he would be able to run like a wild and crazy child around the house. I imagined him using the palm of his hands to inscribe graffiti all over our walls. It would be a symbol of his love. He would then go on, ripping apart our pristine furniture. There then would be the sound of loud banging and ear-shuttering clamor of joy. We would then watch him fall asleep, as we read him bedtime stories. It would be in his bedroom, of course. He would have his own room—Zaire's room. Although Zaire never got to see it, it would be Xavier's secret place of paradise. Time would once again come alive in the hollow room. The wall clock was comatose without its batteries. I had removed them after the doctor had called. Its tick-tock pacing was like a cacophony in my ear. The clock had been frozen in time. But, we were on the cusp of a new season. Xavier and his bright smile would soon come. His alluring laughter lingered in my ears like a haunting melody. He wouldn't talk much, but he liked to laugh. When he was in the mood to talk, however, the usually quiet little boy would turn into a chatterbox. I couldn't always make out what he was trying to say, but it did not matter. Though our daily chats would often lead to a massive telephone bill, we weren't bothered by it. I couldn't wait for Xavier to get home, I told Grace. I couldn't wait for our son to be home.

As the good times continued, Salazar and Capricious seemed to be enjoying our resuscitated bond. They were acting as though we were an extended family. There weren't any more complaints about us not sending enough money for Xavier. Grace was also sending loads of provisions every month. For Xavier's birthday, when he was turning one, Grace sent gifts and treats for a birthday party. Salazar recorded the birthday bash and posted it online.

"Thank God for social media," Grace screamed in excitement.

"Thank God for my kind heart," I said to her, playfully.

It was the phone I had given to him, Salazar told me he used to record the event. I was so angry with him that day in Haiti, when he showed up without Xavier, feeding us a bunch of lies. I thought about taking the phone back. I wished we had been at the party to help Xavier cut his cake. We were still sorting things out with our attorney. Still, everything seemed to be going exactly how we had hoped it would from the beginning. Capricious and I began to develop an intimate bond. She was spearheading—operation Xavier. Anything we needed done, she took care of it. My heart rested in peace, seeing how devoted she was when it comes to her faith. Just about every night, she would carry Xavier to church, she said. "Amazing grace, how sweet the sound," she would sing to me some nights, while we were on the phone. I would sing along, and we would both put Xavier to sleep. "There is a God, praise God!" I said to Grace. How fitting, I thought, for my son to be in the hands of one who shares our faith.

Salazar, on the other hand, seemed to have faded into obscurity. He and I did not talk much, unless it was about the adoption. "Talk to Capricious," he would say to me, if I dared asked anything about Xavier.

I Heard Xavier Cry

I had grown to admire Capricious so much. She had fully regained my trust. She was not shy about telling me how much of an awesome father she thought I was. She would praise me almost daily. "You're a wonderful man, with a beautiful soul," she would say to me. She thanked me endlessly for answering the call to adopt Xavier. She and Salazar were the ones to be admired, I would say to her. They were much more courageous. They had rescued Xavier from the depths of despair. Capricious and her husband were deserving of greater praise. They had vowed to raise Xavier in the presence of God. Unquestionably, it was one of the reasons I had been so quick to forgive. Especially Capricious—although she was pregnant with her own child—her affection for Xavier had not waned. Hence, it was a sad day when she called to tell me the terrible news. It nearly tore me to pieces. She had suffered a miscarriage. It was so depressing to hear; Grace and I were familiar with such pain. It did not discriminate. Though the Good Book had said, death would come to destroy like a thief in the night, it felt worse. The wicked and unpredictable beast had ravaged the womb so mercilessly, leaving its innocent victims without a proper burial.

Capricious wept at the top of her voice. She was flooding in tears.

"Why me, Jude, why me?" she shouted without end.

The heartless monster had waged war against her womb. My heart ached of sorrow; I grew closer to her. The volatile demoiselle was, yet again, in agony.

"It's Xavier, it's because of him," her husband complained.

Capricious had taken a fall, he said, while washing Xavier's clothes. At a loss for words, I stayed quietly on the phone, listening to the brokenhearted couple mourn over the loss of their son. The fury and guilt within me converged. I was at fault, solely to blame for my lack of foresight. My hands were drenched with guilt. The very next day, Grace and I had the couple hire a full-time nanny to help care for Xavier.

Months had passed, we were supposed to return to Haiti for our rescheduled court appointment, but our trip was delayed. Belizaire had traveled out of the country with his wife. She was relocating to France. We were waiting for him to return. As it was taking a long time for Capricious and Salazar to conceive again, they would travel to the Dominican Republic to seek infertility treatment. Their renewed effort in trying to conceive another baby was completely understandable. They were a newly married couple, who had experienced a terrible loss. It all worked out perfectly, nonetheless. Xavier now had a babysitter to look after him while the couple was away. Thankfully, not too long after receiving treatment, Capricious called, singing praises to God. She was pregnant again. "I hope it's twins this time," I said to her. I was so excited for them. However, a ghost of fading memories began to haunt me. After sharing the couple's good news with a longtime friend,

"Have you and Grace tried infertility treatment?" he asked.

I looked at him and let out a deep breath. I did not know what to say. It had crossed our minds a few times, but Grace and I decided against it. His question caught me by surprise. We had been good friends since Grace and I got married; yet he had not once asked.

"God willing," I finally said to him.

"God willing," he repeated.

After the miscarriage, we thought about getting treatment. Nonetheless, we thought adoption was what God wanted for us. We were still young enough, the doctor told us. We had options, he said, since he couldn't find anything wrong. So we chose to wait. We kept hearing God's voice. It was like a faint nudge inside of me; like a soft, prodding wind, urging me to listen to the voice beating my head. It was leading me toward adoption. Perhaps to some, I had given in to folly, but this was the way the heavens designed us to be. Grace felt the same push, the same imposing thrust inside of her. The will of the Almighty was greater than ours. We couldn't resist Him. For who can fight God? Through the journey, nonetheless, God was also about to show us the flaws of many hearts.

With Capricious once again expecting, we were all the more determined to finalize the adoption. She had lost her previous baby while caring for Xavier. Though he had a babysitter for most of the day, Capricious insisted she wanted to be the one to care for most of his needs.

"I'm like a mother to him," she said.

"Don't you kidnap my son now," I playfully said to her.

I sensed the hissing of a soft giggle, but she held her laugh. She and I had become good friends. She told me how unhappy she had been due to her husband's lack of affection.

"He's hardly home nowadays," she said, regarding Salazar.

With a new baby on the way, I'm sure he had to look for work. She was lonely, she said. She desperately needed a friend to share her thoughts. I became that friend in her eyes. Capricious had been

I Heard Xavier Cry

living with her mother-in-law, and it made her miserable.

"Living with her is like living in a den of hell," she said.

"Is it fair to feel like an outcast in my own home?" Capricious uttered with tears.

She yearned for my sympathy; so I gave it to her. The woman sounded as though she was on the verge of a mental breakdown.

"Your words are infectious," she said.

She then started speaking as though honey was coming out of her lips. After a heated argument between me and her husband one evening, Capricious quickly rushed to the phone. She could no longer resist the urge to defend me, she said.

"I don't like the way he talks to you," Capricious confessed.

She stated, she had been holding it in, but could no longer hold her tongue. Her voice was intense, almost as fiery as her husband's shouts had been.

"I will not let him disrespect you," she said.

I told her I didn't need anyone to defend me.

"Loving Xavier the way you do," she said, "I have to defend you."

After the incident, she had me eating out of the palm of her hands as though she had me on a leash. Everything she wanted from me, she received.

When I told Grace, how fond I had become of Capricious, she started to laugh hysterically. But then, it wasn't long before she, as well, would be ensnared by Capriccios' charm. Though she did not put as much faith in Capricious as I did, Grace had moved closer to the shallow ends of Capricious' yawning allure. Grace had spent a ridiculous amount of money one time on a small gift we had sent to Xavier. Capricious pressed her husband to drive nearly three hours to Port- au-Prince to retrieve the box. It had been delivered to the wrong address. The delivery company refused to redeliver the package. They wanted us to pay twice the amount of the initial delivery. At first, Salazar ridiculed Capriccios' request. Driving over three hours for a small gift box, he thought, was insane. Even if he was willing to do it, they did not have a car. He would have to borrow one. He didn't want to take the bus. It would take even longer. I told Capricious she didn't have to go through so much trouble. The box had only a few toys and a small bracelet. Capricious insisted that Salazar recover the package. She had him borrow a car and even gave him money for gas. She knew how much it meant to us. A few days later, she sent us a picture of Xavier wearing the bracelet. "What an awesome woman, Capricious is," I said to Grace. The audacious heroine was not yet done putting her bravery on display.

Salazar, yet again, refused to travel to Port-au-Prince to retrieve another shipment for Xavier. Because the couple lived in such a remote area, it was difficult to get deliveries at their home. Capricious had insisted we send the packages anyway. Salazar had always been the one to retrieve them if they couldn't be delivered. This time, it was another large container, which we usually sent for Xavier every three or four months. The cargo was in a warehouse in Port-au-Prince. Since her husband did not want to travel to get the container, Capricious, then showed her gallant courage. Like a queen on a noble mission, neglecting the nervous tremors inside her womb, she hurtled her way on a bus to get the container. When she got to the warehouse, she had it loaded on top of a bus, she said. That's how she brought it back home. It would be our last time shipping anything for Xavier. Nonetheless, the audacious woman had returned triumphant from her mission. I told her not to do it, but she wouldn't listen to me.

"I did it for you," she said.

She had brought tears to my eyes.

"I told you she can be trusted again," I then began to sing her praises to Grace.

Though she and I had become good friends, Capricious started veering down a path, my instinct found difficult to follow. She began to describe a bizarre family portrait. Neither Salazar, nor Grace were in it.

"Xavier has no one, but you and me," she said.

As I was about to ask to make clear what she meant, my question stopped in midair. I didn't want her to think I was a fool and had assumed the wrong thing. Yet, I could decrypt the thoughts behind her words. She was trying her best to hide them. Her laughter gave her away.

"He only has but you and me," she once again, shamelessly uttered.

The devil had spiced her tongue with myrrh.

"You're such a sweet guy," she said.

"Grace is a wonderful woman and a great mom," I then said to her.

She did not answer. She clammed up with a menacing silence, which I knew would one day return to haunt me. Then, after the bitter pause, her voice soaring with wrath,

I Heard Xavier Cry

"I'm the one caring for Xavier," she said, "not Grace." Our conversation then ended.

KINDRED SPIRITS

I have always been protective of Grace. It has never been a controlling, nor selfish love. It has, and has always been a jealous love, for her sake. It has been that way ever since the day we met. It was a day unlike any other, and I have yet to see anything like it. I had asked God for a piece of silver, but He blessed me with a fine ruby. Grace has been like a jewel, a treasure from Heaven. Though her captivating beauty may be spotted at a glance of her beautiful face, her true beauty lies within. I had prayed to God for the perfect wife; someone with a compassionate heart equal to mine. The thrill of "sowing my wild oats" was quickly fading. It was my prayer request that unforgettable night, seconds before the New Year

I Heard Xavier Cry

would arrive. Finally! The clock had struck midnight; a New Year was upon us.

As I picked up the phone to greet friends and family with well wishes, there was this sweet, angelic voice at the other end of the line. It sounded like a young woman.

"Hello, who is this?' she asked.

I almost hung up. How could this be? I thought.

"Who is this?" I asked.

We continued to shout back and forth, unaware our lines had somehow crossed. We both started to laugh, as we soon realized what had happened. We spoke for hours on end that New Year's night. I didn't want our conversation to end. There was an alluring sweetness in her voice, a zesty blend of guilty pleasure. I started talking funny to her, as if my mind was going through a hypnotic rush. It was just something about the way she made me feel. I couldn't stop even if I wanted to.

"You've got me under your spell," I said to her. "Your voice runs over my ear like a melody."

She wouldn't stop laughing. It was hard for me to keep it together. Her sweet giggles had enticed me even more. She wanted to know why my mouth was so full of honey.

"Why do you talk so sweet to me, when you don't even know me?" she asked.

There was this stirring in my belly, just from hearing her voice.

"You're doing it again," I said.

There was then, a deafening silence on the phone. I knew she didn't hang up. I could hear her breathing heavily. After the awkward pause, I told her,

"This sweet tongue has held you captive for hours, otherwise you would have hung up."

She again covered my ear with her spicy giggle.

"You're too much," she said.

The best was yet to come. We soon discovered, we both had been raised in Haiti. From that moment on, it was no longer a question of *when*, but *where* would we meet.

From then on, it was an early winter evening in Central Park, in New York City. As I approached the clamorous, gridlock street, which would be our meeting place, near 5th avenue and Central Park West. At the congested intersection, stood in the middle of the crowd, the most beautiful girl I had ever seen. Her face radiating a beauty seldom seen in my recollection of beautiful women. She was exceptionally stunning.

My knees started to buckle, the closer I got to her. It was not to the point of lacking confidence, but it was close. Beads of sweat started running down my face. Then, suddenly, it happened. The moment of truth that is. Not having the slightest idea what I looked like, this gorgeous young woman speedily wriggled her way towards me.

"Jude?" she called out, in the same honeyed voice I had heard on the phone.

I didn't even get a chance to answer. She held on to me, our arms interlocking.

"Let's go grab a bite to eat," She said, pulling me closer under the arctic wind.

I knew then, she would be the one. Not even a week later, we had pledged to spend the rest of our lives together. My prayers had been answered.

And so, there we were, more than a decade later, in pursuit of a dream God had placed in our hearts. As I look back to the first day we met, the need to protect Grace from the ills of the world, had always been within me. As we parted ways that day, my heart ached with unease when she walked away. I felt a strong urge to defend her. I didn't know from what. But the longing was coming from a part of me I had never felt before. It was hard to explain. Though I was thrilled to finally meet her, part of me was troubled when she showed up. This was madness, coming out of me. But that's how I felt. It was foolish of her, I thought, to meet me all alone in the vastness of New York City. "What if I had been a predator," I said to her later that evening. Grace thought I was insane. Yet my worries were genuine. It was faith that brought us together. The same faith, which has blessed our union all of these years. I have had an anxious longing to protect Grace since that day. I became her watchman. It is with that zealous love, we traveled the thorn filled journey to Xavier.

Our attorney Belizaire had returned from his trip to France. We had lastly come close to finalizing the adoption. Xavier, nonetheless, would first have to be adopted in Haiti before he could even join us. Yet, even then, he would need a visa to travel. Sailing through the bureaucratic waves of U.S. immigration would not be easy. But once we knew our son was legally ours, the hurdles would be few, leading him to our doorsteps.

While our previous trip to Haiti had been bittersweet, it was essential for us to complete all of the necessary documents on our next visit. We told

I Heard Xavier Cry

Salazar and Capricious about our travel plans. "Tell Xavier, Mommy and Daddy are coming," I urged them. We were again in a rush to see our son. It was nearly six months already since we last saw him. Belizaire had scheduled another court date for us. We weren't sure if we would ever see Xavier again. The adoption threatened to turn into a broken dream. We almost didn't go through with it. Nevertheless, we were going to see him again. To us, he was already our son. That is how we had thought of him. It was the way we had painted him in our hearts. Yet, this is one of the horrors of adoption. The moment we chose to adopt Xavier, we became his mom and dad. It would have been unjust to set aside our emotions until the judge's decree. What a cruel punishment, to both children and parents, to say to them, "cover your heart, find a safe place to hide your love, until it is all over." How can you hide something, which refuses to be tucked away? I say, don't hide your love. Once you have awakened love, can it then withhold its cravings? How distressing, how painful to say to children, "Wait, it's not yet time," as they desperately hunger to be loved. What a travesty it is, to dance on air with love, even if it later brings sorrow of heart.

It is an evil one struggles with when it comes to adoption, the blonde lady at the thrift store had acknowledged. She called it, "an ambiguous upheaval within one's heart." Why does the search for love have to be so difficult, when love claims it has already laid down its arms? Perhaps we will find out when we go to sleep one day. Until the ink legally *dies*, there is no relief in sight. It is likened to a woman who miscarries. The fetus had been part of her. It had become flesh of her flesh. She had safeguarded, loved, and nourished it. *It* belonged to her. *It*, to so many hearts, ferments the soul. *It*, to her, is a scornful word of affection. *It*, was her baby. *It*, was whom her expectant heart had already approved to love, if so chosen. Then, without warning, the abrupt heart-wrenching calmness of her womb causes her to shout louder than the cries of a woman in labor. Grace and I had endured the bitter taste of such misfortune. We were, yet again, poised to wholly commit our hearts to a child, without the privilege of labor pain.

Before leaving for Haiti, I had arranged with Salazar to have all the necessary documents available for our visit. It was coming down to the home stretch. I wanted to avoid any unexpected delays. Salazar had assumed custody of Xavier from Capriccios' sister, Marie-Loraine. She was now enrolled at a university. Thus, she would be too busy with school work, she said. She could no longer help with the adoption.

I Heard Xavier Cry

This time around, Salazar would be the only one traveling with Xavier. With Capricious once again expecting, she decided to stay home. Grace and I wanted to spend quality time with Xavier, so we planned our trip accordingly. Whatever vacation time we had left from work, we took, to allow us to spend more time with our son. We regretted not spending enough time with him on our previous visit. Unlike our first trip, however, which was extremely short, we were going to be in Haiti for close to two weeks. I told Capricious not to pack any clothing for Xavier. Anything he would need when he is with us, we would make sure to bring. Albeit subtle, I sensed some resistance from Salazar when we informed him we would be keeping Xavier until the eve of our last day in Haiti. He sounded terrified. He let out a few heavy sniffs, before asking if we would be able to handle Xavier on our own. He wanted to have someone familiar around, while Xavier was staying with us. I told him we didn't need anyone. I thought it was very insulting of him to ask. If this was his way of expressing concern, out of fear Xavier would be a little nervous, we certainly understood. Even so, Xavier was our son; a chaperone was not needed to look over our shoulders.

"We would like to be with our son alone," I told him, with bottled up anger.

"If you say so," he answered, with what sounded like an irritable chill in his voice.

I knew he was not happy.

RETURN TRIP TO HAITI

Grace and I arrived in Haiti on a beautiful sunny afternoon. We were immediately greeted by the scorching heat of midafternoon. We were so excited to be home again. The sweltering heat, and bombast of folkloric tunes, brought back memories of our last visit. Unlike our last trip home, however, Grace and I weren't as nervous. We wanted to explore more of the islands' hidden beauty. Its humble spirit following the earthquake had given way to a forceful resurgence. Certainly, many were still struggling to survive in the midst of this period of recovery. However, the resolve of the Haitian people had not been defeated. Haiti was still a beautiful place, a paradigm of an island paradise. It was saturated with an abundance of delightful cuisine, sweet melodies, and charismatic people. And yet, we could not close our eyes to the constraining poverty plaguing its people. It brought us a lot of grief, to see many children and their families still living in makeshift tents out on the streets. The woeful sights reminded me why Grace and I had been so willing in giving of ourselves. It was, after all, the unsung cry of these nameless children that ignited our call to action. Xavier's desperate cry for love from underneath the rubble would be the one in fate's eyes.

There had been so much built up anticipation leading up to our trip. I'm not sure if it was because Xavier was so close to legally becoming our son or just the thought of us seeing him again. There was something about this particular visit, destined to be special. Later in the afternoon after our arrival, we were picked up at the airport by Grace's aunt. We had planned on spending the night at her house, before heading to the province of Jacmel, the next day. Salazar was going to drop off Xavier at the house later that evening. Remembering all too well the friction it had once created, Grace and I, yet again, paid roundtrip airfare for Salazar and Xavier to travel. This time, we had the itinerary confirmation forwarded to us. While the roads were vastly improved, according to Salazar, we felt that Xavier was still too young to travel by bus. The extra cost was worth the sacrifice.

I Heard Xavier Cry

We arrived at Grace's aunt's house with drum rolls beating in my chest. I was restless, desperately wanting to see Xavier. After a quick nap, Grace and I sat on the second floor on top of the steps overlooking the street. A few family friends gathered around, talking to me. Yet, the more they talked, the more their voices seemed to fade out. I was running out of patience. My long, unending wait to see my son, was taking too long. I kept such a close watch on what was going on outside; every passing car was being stored in my memory. *Where are they already?* I kept thinking. A short time later, as I made my way farther out to the balcony, I looked down and noticed this chubby looking boy with corn rolls. He was walking as though he owned the streets. He hovered his way past our corridor, whirling his head around. Not too far behind was Salazar, strolling as though he were in deep thoughts.

"My son has finally arrived," I shouted to myself, wondering how he was going to react seeing me.

I then slowly strutted my way down the steps.

"Hey!" I yelled out in surprise.

Xavier was already standing at the bottom of the steps waiting for me. He had this curious look on his face. He stared at me until I had reached the bottom step. He then stood motionless in front of me, twirling his fingers with both hands at his side. Without uttering a word, he lifted his head, welcoming me with a hasty smile. It shot right into my chest. By now, Salazar had caught up to us, forcefully taking hold of Xavier by the hand. He then followed behind me, walking so tentatively with Xavier. My son looked so much different face to face. From the way he kept looking at me, he probably thought the same thing. As we headed inside, Xavier continued to keep a watchful eye on me. Once in a while, I would look back to see why Salazar was being so tentative, but I would end up locking eyes with Xavier. He and I would sometimes video chat, so I knew he had remembered me. Nevertheless, there was something about me prompting his curious gaze.

Once inside the house, Xavier sat on Salazar's lap. While Salazar and I were talking, Xavier extended his arms, trying to reach for me, as he was being clutched by a firm grasp. I wondered if he had been impatiently waiting for me to hold him. This was my son, but I had failed to return the same eagerness he had shown me. Through it was a quiet enthusiasm, I saw it in his eyes. They were telling me, "Here I am, Daddy." I was just waiting. I'm not sure for what, but I waited. Perhaps, it was because my spirit was speaking to me. Children are like sponges, they can absorb almost

I Heard Xavier Cry

anything. So if my son thought something was wrong, he was probably dead-on. Though the zeal of a proud father, anxious to bond with his first child may not have been so obvious, I was dying to hold my son. Still, the menacing thoughts would not go away. What my eyes were witnessing could not be ignored. As much as I wanted it to, my instinct was not about to deceive me.

Xavier, again, had both arms drawn-out, eagerly waiting on me to take hold of him. Salazar held him back. Thinking it might have simply been a spontaneous gaffe, I called out to Xavier, hoping my son would reach for his daddy's hands. And he did. But even then, Salazar held on to him with a firm grip. It looked as though he was doing it on purpose. I could see the tension in the muscles around his neck, desperately struggling with himself not to let go of Xavier.

"Come to Daddy," I, once again, said to Xavier; my hands stayed up this time.

I was flapping both hands for him to come to me. With both of my hands on hold in midair, I was convinced they were not going to return void. Xavier must have read my mind. At least I thought he did. He wrestled his way out of Salazar's stubborn grip. He then climbed on my lap and pressed his face against my lips. He smiled at the warmth of a father's gentle kiss. My son then began to laugh mercilessly. He thought it was funny. He turned his head back, sticking his tongue out at Salazar.

"Have you no shame?" Salazar said to my baby boy, sounding annoyed.

Salazar tried to grab him from me, but Xavier kept pushing his hands away. While Salazar acted as though it was all fun and games, I knew better. The playful tug-of-war over my son seemed to have bothered him. His lips appeared to be quivering with contempt. My son had not dishonored me in the battle of the wills.

Not a moment too soon, Grace, who had been delayed, finally entered the room. She had a huge grin on her face when she saw Xavier sitting on my lap. He had such a firm grip of my shirt, one would have thought it was a desperate plea to never let him go.

"There goes your boy," I said to Grace, as I handed Xavier to her.

She held him close to her chest, while she gazed into his eyes. She starred at him for so long, her eyes stood still, as though she were looking right through him. Her smile had disappeared, leaving behind a faceless excitement. The room was soundless. Perhaps that's all my mind wanted me to hear—the dense stillness of a mother's love. For all I could hear was the soft wisp of air coming out of my nostrils. I looked at Salazar—he, as well, seemed lost in the moment. Mother and Son, were on stage, pouring out their hearts for the world to see. Whatever treasure trove Grace was hoping to discover, she had found. Xavier cuddled her face with both hands. He then leaned over and gave her a kiss on her lips. Teardrops started spilling out of her eyes. My eyes were also full of tears. Salazar looked downcast. His eyes pink as a somber sky. His cry looked like a cry of anguish.

The precious moment was short-lived. From nowhere, Salazar started shouting at Xavier.

"Come get your juice, little boy," he said.

Grace, then quietly placed Xavier on my lap. I had taken his bottle from Salazar. Xavier pushed the bottle away, shaking his head restlessly as I was trying to feed it to him. He then crouched over my lap, turning his back to Salazar.

"Xavier!" Salazar screamed out once more.

Though Xavier was ignoring him, Salazar continued to call his name.

"I see you're all over Uncle Jude," Salazar, then said to Xavier.

"*Uncle!*"

It must have been a slipup. And yet, it sounded more like a curse, an angry word. It felt as though he had shot a bullet filled with insults at me.

It did not take too long to realize, Salazar's slip of the tongue was no mistake. It was said with malicious intent. While Xavier rested on my lap, Salazar decided it was time to leave. As he was on his way out, his eyes were once again moist and red. They appeared to be soaking with grief. He picked up Xavier to kiss him goodbye, trying his best to hold back his tears. He looked like a stubborn father with a heavy heart. He then said to Xavier, "Are you leaving with me?" He might have acted as though it were a playful request, but my ears heard differently. I heard a cunning man, trying to lure my son out of the door. I also saw a man, whose spirit seemed to have been crushed. Unsure whether they had prepared Xavier for the visit, since he and Capricious assured me they would, I grabbed Xavier by the arm, with Salazar still holding on to him.

"You're staying with me," I said to him.

He turned his head, smiling at Salazar. His laughter was met with a cold stare. Xavier then bowed his head to the floor. He looked sad.

"Let me go, let me go," Xavier then cried out.

He was trapped in the crossfire of two desperate men. Although I acted as if I was tone-deaf to my son's words, it was out of fear that they were perhaps being hurled at me. What was echoing out of his lips had trampled my spirit. Was my son rejecting me? His fiery words threatened to turn a proud father into a wounded warrior.

"Let me go!" Xavier, yet again, pleaded.

Salazar, seizing the opportunity shrewdly added,

"See, he wants to go home."

Things were not going well. While I reasoned with myself to understand why Salazar found it difficult to leave Xavier behind, I fought harder to defend my own cause. Salazar had practically raised him from birth. Nevertheless, I had been his loving dad for just as long. My heart had been linked to his and his to mine. Regardless of how I had come to love him so much, I did. He was my son.

Fortunately, the hands of Grace intervened once more. God had always worked through her. She had witnessed a battle of the wills between two unwavering fathers. She would now have to play the role of an arbitrator. Grace always played fair. But this time, I did not want her to. I knew she was not going to force Xavier to stay if he didn't want to. Yet, deep down inside, I had faith, my honorable queen would not disappoint me. Though she would be a fair judge, Grace wouldn't allow the silent cries within me to be put to shame. I trusted her, just as much as I trust in God. Though it was an unfair burden to place on any living soul, Grace had always managed to come through. Perfection was never what I sought from her. It was her love; the way her heart had covered me with undying devotion. Just as my life was in God's hands, my heart belonged to her.

And so, the three of us watched with restless anticipation as the heart that had loved me after all of these years was about to display her grace. Salazar was holding Xavier in his arms, while Xavier had his small hands bound into mine. Grace walked towards us, bouncing every step with the relish of a confident mother.

"Come here baby," she called out to Xavier.

He writhed his way out of my hand, and Salazar's tight grip, then slid right into the arms of Grace. She put Xavier down, took him by the hand, and walked away.

"He will be okay," she said.

The love of my life had done it again. I wanted to laugh, but my spirit resisted. My mind was struggling to remain calm amidst the awkwardness of the moment.

After Salazar had left, I went out to the balcony where Xavier was running around with the other children in the house. He seemed to be having a wonderful time. Whenever he would come near me, he would stop to look at me and offer a smile. He was a handsome boy, with an unforgettable "Million dollar" smile. Everyone started calling him "XZ." He spent the rest of the evening being entertained by the other children. Being the new kid on the block, he had them spellbound. Grace and I gave him space to roam around the house as he pleased. Every so often, he would come looking for us. He would then let out a few deep breaths with a grin on his face. It was as though he wanted to let out heavy breaths of relief after he had found us. We were his place of sanctuary. He would check-in, give both of us a kiss, then go out to play.

That night, with the whole house in their usual nighttime worship, Xavier fell asleep in my arms. Grace stared at us throughout the prayer. She had a sad look on her face. She didn't have to say anything. There had also been an aching in my spirit. No matter how much I tried to shake it off, it wouldn't go away.

Jude Emmanuel

The way Salazar had acted stirred an intense haze of uncertainty in me. Whatever the outcome would be, we were courageous enough to accept it. Yet, the fear was in the ambiguity of it all. "God, my heart lies before you like an open book. Open my eyes, so that I may see. And if it is blindly open to love, open my heart, so it too may see. Don't let me lose my son," I prayed to the Good Lord.

Though I prayed, the fury within me remained. It was a silent rage, which refused to go away. So, as I observed the love of my life, seemingly downhearted, the possibility of me losing my son began to haunt my spirit. While the prayer was ending, I turned to look at Xavier, whose eyes were now wide open. He looked at me and stared with a frown. I then kissed him on the forehead, and said, "Father, good or bad, may your will be done."

The following morning, the entire family set out to travel to Grace's hometown of Jacmel. The exquisite architectural province is located roughly fifty-five miles south of the capital. We did not get a chance to visit Jacmel on our last visit, but Grace insisted on visiting her grandfather and other family members living in Jacmel. Grace had been raised in the small province. Her profound affection of its majestic serenity was something she had always talked about. I had never once visited any of the provinces when I was growing up in Haiti. Grace had promised to one day take me to Jacmel. It would be an experience of a lifetime, she told me. With Xavier on board for the trip, it felt as if we were heading to the Promised Land.

We woke up early in the morning, as it was habitually done with Grace's family before departing for a long trip. The enchanted melody of the roosters seemed to rise with every breath I inhaled. We all ate breakfast and boarded a commercial bus on our way to Jacmel. Grace and I sat in the back of the bus. It was sweltering hot and the humidity close to unbearable. On the other hand, we were having a splendid time on the road. One of Grace's cousins, Jonathan, whom Xavier had become very fond of, also sat in the back. Xavier sat on his lap. Jonathan was the one who started calling Xavier "XZ." He was much older than Xavier. Jonathan was having trouble saying Xavier's name, so he uttered whatever came naturally. We all thought it was a cool name; so everyone else stared calling Xavier by that name. Jonathan was a bright and compassionate kid. He was a lot like Xavier, children with big hearts. They were more than willing to share their snacks with the other kids on the bus. Xavier liked him a whole lot. He and Jonathan were inseparable back at the house. He was the only one

Xavier would allow to feed him, other than me and Grace. We also saw in him, what Xavier was able to discern. Jonathan's parents had ten children. His parents could not afford to raise them all on their own, so some of the kids were sent to live with various family members. Jonathan was one of them. He and his younger brother were being raised by Grace's aunt. He always spoke with candor. "I know we're poor," he said. Yet, he seldom apologized for his parents' enormous sacrifice. He was determined not to use it as an excuse for not succeeding in life. His gentle nature took me back to an uncomfortable place. One, which had been buried deep within my conscience. Jonathan was family, while Xavier was not. That's how it was perceived through the lenses of our family. Still, Xavier was my son, and I loved him. Nevertheless, every time I would look at Jonathan, it impelled me to once again ask myself, *why not him?*

The road to Jacmel unveiled the most breathtaking sights—a gorgeous quiet, but not necessarily the most comfortable. Driving up the steep mountains provided an aesthetic climb into paradise. At times it felt as if our lives were hanging by a thread or at the mercy of the driver. I was one of the few who seemed to worry about our safety. Everyone else appeared to be enjoying every moment, including Xavier. He was having so much fun, shouting at the top of his lungs, as though he were enjoying a fantasy ride at an amusement park. It took us almost two hours before we finally arrived at Grace's grandfather's home. This was my first time meeting him, along with many of Grace's other family members. Grace had a lot of relatives living in Jacmel. They were extremely amusing and hospitable. One of the first things that surprised me was the countless young children in the family. Grace had talked about having a lot of young cousins living in Haiti, but they had far outnumbered my expectation. We thought about adopting one or two of these children, but they all had parents. The more time we spent with these children, the more, guilt had wrapped itself around me like an iron quilt. While I delighted in having these children around, it had also carried discomfort. Any torment of remorse would have to wait until my boy had come home. Perhaps we would adopt one of these children after Xavier had come home, I told Grace. Our trip to Jacmel, nonetheless, was about Xavier. It was about finally spending alone time with our son in paradise.

Around dinner time, as we all gathered at the table, someone enquired about Xavier,

"Hey, Jude, who's this little boy?" the man asked.

It was an older gentleman, a friend of the family. For a moment, I did not know how to respond. Grace turned to me with an odd look, perhaps, wanting to know why it was taking me so long to answer. The man then persisted,

"Is he your son? He looks like you," he said.

I was about to tell him, Xavier was indeed my son. But then, one of Grace's aunts said to him, "that's his nephew."

It suddenly dawned on me, many in Grace's family had been unaware who Xavier truly was. They knew he was going to be adopted. Conversely, they had assumed he was from my side of the family. And, just as it was with my family, a lot of them were curious. They wanted to know *why*, thinking Xavier was part of Grace's family. *Why not*, I thought.

At times, I wondered if the orphan cry I had heard in my head was the voice of Zaire, calling me from his secret place. He had departed in the end without a father. And I was left without a son. But, it was never my dead son speaking in my head. It was that other Spirit. The *One*, whom my soul rested in its hands. The *One*, who leads all, even against their own will. I wished for that Spirit to enlighten me. I felt trapped within my own walls. Why did I even care about people's sorry cynicism? "Answer me," I cried out to the Holy Spirit. I was never afraid to stand before any

I Heard Xavier Cry

living creature and stare at them straight in the eyes. But love had broken down my iron will. I started caring too much. why was a once prideful man feelimg so torn and broken ? I pleaded with the Spirit to tell me.

My heart began to throb violently, nearly bursting with anger. I couldn't believe what I was hearing. One of Grace's cousins had approached me while taking Xavier for a walk after dinner. "You know," she said, "some people think he's your son." I gasped through a nervous laugh. Of course he's my son, I thought. For God' sake, he was going to be adopted. That's not what she meant. Many of them thought Xavier was a love child from another woman. I was trying to cover up my indiscretion they said.

"What indiscretion?" I asked the young woman. "They are but empty words," I told her.

She went on to tell me, a lot of people were asking why I was playing the role of a preacher man, while at the same time trying to hide a grave sin. These vicious character assassinations were nothing new. It reminded me of the time when Grace and I had just said our vows. A week later, right in the middle of a church service, a good friend told us, she heard we were getting a divorce. It felt as if somebody was waging a war to destroy us. Our integrity was being demolished in the bloodbath, but we let it go. The rumors, and the whispers, weren't always so obscure. Though I hadn't traveled to Haiti before our last visit, one of my uncles had confronted me. Uncle Willie was a man of God, a pastor at a Pentecostal church in New York City. When he heard Xavier looked a lot like me, he asked if I had committed adultery. He thought I had been with another woman visiting from Haiti.

"Son," he said, sounding as though he was about to preach. "Grace is a sweet girl now, you hear," Uncle Willie said.

Although we were speaking on the phone, I imagined him standing with the phone in his left hand, and his right arm raised up, pointing to the sky as he normally did before a sermon. Uncle Willie knew better. He had seen how God had unveiled my heart to the world. Not that I was invulnerable to sin, but if it were true, he knew I would tell him. Hence, he ended our talk that day with the same words of wisdom he had always preached. "Though he may slay me, yet I will trust in him."

As if I wasn't worn-out enough from the scolding of my own relatives, the wall of cynicism had even followed me to Jacmel. Our first night, I unexpectedly walked in on this young woman interrogating Xavier.

She was fishing to discover if Xavier was my biological son.

"Little boy, who's your daddy?" the young lady repeatedly asked as I was about to enter the room.

I stood quietly outside the door to listen. She had her back to the door, while Xavier arched on her lap.

"Tell me, who's your daddy?" She continued to probe.

"Jude? 'Is it Jude?" she asked once more.

By then, Xavier's eyes had landed outside of the door. He looked up, pointed at me, and pulled back his cheeks with a smile. When the young woman turned around to see who Xavier was looking at, and saw it was me, her eyes lit up. She let out a loud scream, as though she had seen a ghost.

"You!" she said, thinking she had uncovered a forbidden family secret. It did not matter if she thought Xavier was my son from another woman. The word had already flooded the streets like a band of Mardi-Gras on a carnival strip.

As the awkward rumors began to flare up, Grace and I wished we had kept the adoption private. We knew eventually the whole world would find out. But, why was my heart feeling so bitter. The mayhem made my soul groan. Perhaps, it was because of my own guilt. I worried too much about trying to keep everyone happy—both sides of the family that is. Deep down, I knew why there were so many questions. It had nothing to do with me having an illegitimate child. It was about resentment. I was fearful of it from the beginning. Though no one said a word, I knew they were blinded by jealousy. It would have been better if Xavier were instead a child conceived out of my sinful lust. Then, no one would really care. But since we were adopting a child unknown to both families, the steels of bitterness had been erected against us. Yet, Xavier was already my son, my adopted son.

With our tour of Jamel just beginning, Grace wanted us to have a good time with Xavier. We needed to enjoy every second together as though it were our last, she said. Everyone treated Xavier like royalty, as if he wore a crown over his head. Since there was not enough space at the table during meal time, Xavier sat at the table with us, while the other children sat on the floor. Grace's aunt would have him sit at the head of the table, facing me. Though they had served us like royal guests, it made me feel uncomfortable. At night, Xavier slept on the bed with us, while the rest of the children slept on the floor. The guilt which once again was tormenting me had threatened to come out.

After only a couple of days in Jacmel, we had gotten to know a whole lot about Xavier. He was very smart for a kid his age. By this time, he was only a year and a half, but he had the zeal of a much older child. It was his survival spirit, I thought. It made him grow up fast. Children around his age were surprisingly bright, I had learned. But with Xavier, his charisma was unlike any other. My heart ached with sorrow sometimes when I would look at him. I then would wonder if I had discovered the ghost of my dead son. If he were such treasure, I had found it. He stirred up our hearts and made us laugh. He had even made us cry good tears, weeping of joy. We had hoped our eyes would never see the day of bitter tears for our son.

Xavier loved Grace. He would often run after her, following her every move. There were a lot of steep hills and a rugged looking mountain near the house. Every time I would ask Grace to go on a hike, Xavier would throw a tantrum and pull her away. "No," he would say to her, "bad, bad," with a frightened look on his face. He had come a long way since the earthquake. Death had almost captured him, but it was not yet his day. Both of his parents were gone.

And yet, he didn't know it. He was only a month old when it happened. I wondered if their faces had been imprinted somewhere in his mind. When I was growing up in Haiti, my aunt used to tell me, once a baby nourishes from a breast, the one who feeds is never forgotten. Xavier had perhaps, tasted his mother's love, and now was craving Grace's love. The three of us went everywhere together. We roamed through the tall grasses, as we marveled at the tree lines and their magnificent beauty. There were a lot of animal farms along the road. Most evenings, and sometimes late at night, we would all go swimming. Grace and Xavier loved being in the water. As for me, taking refuge under a mango tree, while devouring its fruits was far more than paradise. Xavier wasn't too fond of mangos. He had rather sipped on coconut juice. In the afternoon, we would carry coconuts with us before heading to the beach. We were careful not to give him too much. We were told it could upset his stomach. He kept on asking for more. Grace never indulged him. She would simply tell him, "no more." Xavier did not like to disappoint her. When she gave him a snack he didn't care to eat, he would hide it or give it to me. It was always when Grace was not looking. She got very angry with me after I had done it a few times. "This is not the way you raise a child," she said. I knew it was wrong; I was just having fun with my son.

I Heard Xavier Cry

One afternoon, the family took us to visit one of their neighbors who lived a few blocks from the house. She had been a close friend of the family for years. She and her husband had six young children, four boys and two girls. Sophia, the youngest child was two and a half years old. She was a pretty little girl, with the spirit of a movie star. As soon as we walked into the house, she started following me around. At one point, she held on to my hand and wouldn't let go. After a few hours of us running around on the playground, we came back in the house to the tune of the little girl calling me "Daddy." Perhaps it was crazy of me to think she was a bit overzealous, as her attachment to me seemed a little premature. It was her first time meeting me. I started to wonder what in the world was going on. Her mom, also had joined in the act, "Daddy, Daddy," she started cheering me on, prompting her daughter to do the same. The calculating serenade seemed awkward. I played along, but I knew there was more to it. The little girl wasn't to blame. She was only doing what her mother told her to. But why? Was the house full of cheer to welcome a new daddy? Or was it a joyful ruse to suffocate me with guilt?

Later in the afternoon, as the little girl's mother and I rested on her front porch, we began to chat. She then offered me a shot of Haitian rum. We both sat on the floor, underneath the tropical breeze.

"So, Jude, why him?" she asked. "He's not family."

Although sipping rum was not a habit, since she offered it to me, I indulged. She called it— medicine for the heart. By now, however, my head and my chest started to feel warm. Whether it was because of the alcohol, or her offensive remark, my chest started to burn like a raging fire. If her so-called medicine had been a ploy to help scour my thoughts, it had the opposite effect. It made me sick to my stomach.

"He's an orphan," I said to her.

She then looked at me square in the eyes, poured me another shot, and took a deep breath into the sky. It was what I had feared the most. Though no one in the family openly protested, the little girl's mother had objected on their behalf. It would be blasphemous to say that we didn't care. We did. But if we were to adopt from family, as we had planned after Xavier had come home, who would it be? And from which side of the family? No matter who we decided to adopt, there was sure to be grumbling between both families. I wasn't always sure why we cared, but we did. It felt as if we were being strangled by the same love that had ignited our journey. It was like having our own fists pressed against our chests, like a dart, shot out of Cupid's bow.

We had been frozen in time when we first got to Jacmel. At least, that's what it felt like. Now, the days were flying away as if they were reluctant to be engraved in our memory. "Good days, good days," I said with regard to the time we were spending with our son. One day, Xavier and I played kickball under the scorching afternoon sun, for what seemed like hours. Since we could not find a real soccer ball to play with, we used a crushed-up soda can. It brought me back to the days as a child growing up in Haiti. If there weren't any kick balls around, we used whatever we could find and turned it into a soccer ball. That's how the kids in the neighborhood used to do it. Though the passage of time had betrayed my youthful bliss, as everyone kept teasing me, Xavier loved it. He and I demolished the aluminum can with a volley of free kicks, until it nearly shattered into pieces. Thank God we were wearing sneakers. Sometimes, we used to play with our foot bare when I was a kid. With fatigue settling in, it was time for us to take a break. I was so exhausted, both of my hands resting on my waist, I struggled to breathe. Xavier kept his eyes on me the whole time. Then, he too, placed both of his hands at his side.

"Xavier, are you all right?" I asked, gasping for air.

He then ran towards me,

"Daddy," he yelled out with his winsome smile.

It was the first time he had ever called me dad since we had been in Jacmel.

"I love you, son," I said to him, after I had picked him up and gave him a daddy's kiss on his forehead.

I remember trying to put on his diaper one day. It felt awkward doing it for the first time. Xavier kept looking at me. He had his eyes fixed into my own, after I had let out a few huffs of frustration. It may have looked a bit odd to him, not knowing what I was doing. He began to laugh when he saw it was taking too long. I wondered if that's how most dads felt, changing their children's diaper for the first time. Although it smelled like raw sewage, it might as well had been cheap cologne. It didn't bother me at all. After I had struggled to put it on, Xavier laughed, applauding with a fist pumped in the air. That's when I heard Grace's sweet laughter behind me. She had been watching the whole time; her mouth muzzled with both hands. "Don't be embarrassed," she said. I wasn't, my son had cheered me on.

Xavier loved being in the water. Whenever we were too tired to go far out to the shore, we would take him

I Heard Xavier Cry

to the ravine nearby. He only wanted Grace to carry him. He would sit in the water for a long time, looking as though he was meditating. At night, the three of us would sit outside on the porch, mimicking the sounds of crickets.

"Cricket cry, cricket cry," Xavier would sing in the dusky hours of the night.

He was not afraid of the dark. He loved to play the hiding game, as twilight loomed, using the pungent darkness as cover. Though the dark skies had threatened to capture his soul and make him disappear the night of the earthquake, he had overcome its fright. One can only imagine the ghastly horror his eyes had witnessed. He would hide alone in the dark. When it was time for us to find him, "Mama! Papa!" he would shout behind the bushes, as though he had seen the shadows of the souls who had given him birth. There would be a strange throbbing in his voice. He then would come out of his hiding place with a smiley face, yet with droplets of tears rolling softly down his cheeks. When asked if something had hurt, "yes," he would cry out with a stream of mysterious tears. Xavier loved the hiding game. But he could never tell us where it hurts. We stopped playing that game. "Kache, Kache, (Hide, hide,)" he would plead with us to play. We were afraid it would hurt again. Though Grace and I resisted yielding to the reality of his world, we soon realized, his grief and love of the night had become friends.

Xavier ran after Grace, as though she were candy cane. He sought after her love, as if it were the place where his spirit had found comfort. Yet, he had made sure not to brush aside my love. One night, as we were getting ready to go to sleep, he crawled in between the two of us. He put his arms around Grace, as though he wanted to carry her away. He firmly held on to her, gingerly stroking her face. With his back facing me, his right hand cuddling Grace, he reached back with his left hand and began to run his tiny fingers over my face. What an awesome kid, I thought. But he wasn't yet done with me. He then turned, facing me, and rubbed his nose on my face. "Love you, Daddy," he whispered in my ear. Grace had taught him how to say it. I would have given the world to bring him home with us that night.

The next morning, against Xavier's wishes, Grace and I decided it was time to take a hike up the beautiful mountain near the house. Xavier wanted Grace to stay back with him. But since Jonathan, and the other children wanted to join us, Xavier changed his mind. He tried so desperately to have Grace carry him. She could not bear it. One of Grace's cousins offered to take him up. Somehow, Xavier had figured out I would not be able to carry him all the way to the top. From time to time, I would take him from Grace's cousin and put him on my back. But after a while, he knew the tough hike had robbed me of all my strength. Someone else had to bring him up the rest of the way. Half way through the hike, I was like a dead man walking. It took us about an hour and a half to make it all the way up the mountain. When we had finally reached the top, most of us crouched on our knees with exhaustion. I wished life beyond the mountain was as beautiful as its view from the mountain top. The countryside, the real beauty of Jacmel, had been revealed. The scenic plains, openly bared their sacred mass of serenity. We had ascended to what we envisioned Heaven would be like. There we were, on top of the world, lounging in our secret paradise. We had spent nearly two weeks without the use of the internet, cell phones, or television. I had come to understand the world Grace forever raved about. She loved nature, and it was where she found peace.

"Do you think, Heaven is as beautiful as this?" she asked, as she, Xavier, and I huddled together in a warm embrace.

I had not a clue what Heaven looks like. Still,

"Yes, yes sweetie," I said to Grace. "It sure feels like Heaven."

It was the Promised Land I had imagined.

While going up the mountain felt like running through a long-drawn-out course, without an end, our descent had triggered the same dent of will. As it started to rain a little, we had to go down a different path. It was much safer, yet so small. Everyone, except the young children, had to swivel their way down the narrow hill. As I had been the last one to make it up the mountain, I was the last one down. The hike up the hills had been exhilarating. But now, the adrenaline-charged, the thrill of being on top of the world, were all quickly fading. There was this huge knot in my stomach. The rush of excitement had come to an end. It was the evening before returning to Port-au-Prince. Before Xavier would return to Salazar and Capricious. Suddenly, the mango and coconut leaves had lost their fragrance. The ocean's aquatic bliss had disappeared. Jacmel had lost its appeal. It had been stripped of its beauty. The uncertainty in not knowing what was going to happen with our son weighed heavily in our minds. Xavier would soon legally become our son. And yet, the chances of us ever seeing that day seemed grim. I had seen the deep end of the journey in Salazar's eyes.

I Heard Xavier Cry

"Good morning," the bus driver greeted me the next day.

He showed up two hours earlier than expected. Time was moving as though it had given in to the haste of destiny.

"Good morning to you," I replied.

Yet, it wasn't a good morning. It didn't feel like the day was going to let my mind rest. Fear and love were together wrestling in my head. We were on our way back to Port-au-Prince. Xavier was getting ready to return home. "I will fight for you," I said to him. He sat on my lap during the entire ride back to the house. His head resting on my chest, he would nervously coil his fingers into mine. He knew he was going home. His eyes stood erect, staring through the cracks on top of the bus. Every so often, a flicker of sunshine would light up his face. He would then stare back at it with a blank stare. My son knew he was going home. I tried to get him to smile, but he wouldn't. I wondered what was going through his mind. When he had finally turned to look at me, I saw the sad look on his face. I suddenly felt a sharp pain in my chest. It felt as though my ribs had been hit with a brick. "What's wrong, Xavier?" I kept asking. He would not answer. He did not even want to finish his breakfast. Grace sat across from us. She seldom looked our way. Her eyes were shut for most of the ride. The mood inside the bus was one of silent gloom. The soft humming of gospel hymns from Grace's aunt was all one could hear. Everyone else had been held captive by the stillness of the moment. Even the children looked as though they were lost in space. Perhaps, Grace's aunt had lured them to sleep with her harmonizing chorus. Nonetheless, my heart was beginning to feel empty. My love for my son was being overpowered by fear. "Be brave, man of God," I let out to myself, even though I felt powerless. I used to be a selfish creature, I thought. My heart had once been shielded by iron shafts. It had now been freed of its rugged edges. What in the world was happening to me? It was because of the Spirit. The Holy Spirit had changed me. I had often felt like a mighty warrior when my will had its own wings. But ever since I submitted, and began to live with a new heart, it felt as though my own will had been crushed. My backbone had crumbled into pieces. Just as my lament was about to end, "Nou rive Nou rive (we're here, we're here)" the bus driver shouted. Grace was tapping me on the shoulder. I had apparently fallen asleep.

We made it back to the house close to the middle of the day. Everyone looked exhausted from the long ride. Grace and I went to our room with Xavier, trying to get him to take a nap. He didn't want to. Grace gave him something to eat, then went to sleep. If her heart had been weeping, she did not show it. Then again, she didn't have to. Overwhelmed with anxiety, I nonetheless, was eagerly looking forward to our court appointment the following day. I called Salazar to remind him of our court date. He didn't have a lot to say. His words were brief, and cold, almost like the sound of bitterness. He denied it when asked if he harbored any resentment towards me because of Xavier. There was nothing for him to be hostile about, he said. Yet, his voice quivered with the spite of a bitter man.

It didn't cross my mind until we had left Jacmel, but it would take another court appearance before the adoption would be finalized. We were going to court, only to file our "intent to adopt" document. It was a momentous day for us. We would be one step closer, a few signatures away, before the anxiety would be cast away. Fear had been mounting. We didn't want to lose our son. We couldn't walk away, could we? Our love had been stretched across the Caribbean Sea. Love and fear were becoming the same. Grace felt as though she was going through labor on the eve of our court date.

"Love doesn't always deliver what it promises," she reminded me that evening.

"I know, sweetie. Trust me, I know," I said to her, understanding that love had once failed to come through.

However, love is always faithful, isn't it? It can never be defeated, I told her. If God is love, and love doesn't work out, then it must not have been written in His will. We were praying that our spirit wouldn't get crushed again. We were getting close, closer than Zaire had been, but not far along enough for our hearts to be at peace. We would still be filled with grief. Anguish would still rest in our bed. The next day, the day of our court date, would also be our last day in Haiti. The last day we would get to spend with Xavier. Though we wanted to bring him home with us, he wasn't yet ready to come. I heard Xavier's cry that night. I saw our son crying.

"Look! He's crying," I screamed out to Grace, waking her up from a deep sleep. But when she turned to look at Xavier, he was sound asleep. Was I hallucinating?

"It well might have been," Grace said. She thought I may have been dreaming with my eyes wide-shut.

At the dawn of a new day, echoed once again the chorus of roosters. They were crowing a happy song, a hymn of grace, a crow of praise. It was indeed the day that the Lord had made. That particular day, however, my usual morning prayer was overshadowed by doubt. God had been pulling me closer to Him. Thus, I was at the height of a spiritual transformation. It started the day Grace and I met on the phone. A decade had passed since that fateful New Year's Day. God had been shaping and molding me. Hence, at the time of my morning prayer before leaving for the courthouse, I could not have been any closer to the righteous Spirit. And yet, my own spirit had grown weak while in prayer that morning. My heart groaned, and my spirit started to grumble once again. How could that be? Words from the Good Book, once again began to canvass my mind. They seemed contrary to what I thought our assignment was to be. Had God changed His mind?

Grace and I couldn't even finish our breakfast. Xavier woke up with a happy face, but it did not last long. As soon as we were on our way out of the door, his demeanor had changed. Perhaps, he thought he was going back home. We arrived at the courthouse late morning, along with our attorney, Belizaire. Salazar showed up a few minutes later. He had a strange expression on his face. He looked as though he had been soaked with regret. Standing before me, was a soul, who no doubt had been on edge. As soon as he saw Xavier, his pale expression turned into willful joy.

Xavier did not want to go anywhere near him. My cousin Mario, his wife, and several other family witnesses were present for the declaration of our intent to adopt. Before our meeting with the judge, I approached Salazar, and pleaded with him one last time to see if he had changed his mind about the adoption. It was just the two of us chatting outside on the steps of the courthouse.

"I have my own son on the way," he said.

Still, his words were not in tune with the sadness on his face.

"Don't make us waste our time," I told him.

He didn't say a word. He simply looked back at me with an empty stare. As we were heading back inside,

"Young man! Come here," someone yelled out to me.

When I turned around, I noticed it was the crippled man who had been napping outside of the courthouse. He had a few grey hair and wisdom lines on his face. He looked as though he had been a soldier in his youthful years. He was missing one of his legs. I took out a few dollars out of my pocket to give to him. He took a quick glance at the cash and put it in the empty plastic jar next to him.

"Young man," he said, "Trust your pain, it doesn't lie."

I Heard Xavier Cry

As I was about to ask, what on God's earth his words had to do with me, one of the court employees came to get me.

"Mr. Villard, you're needed inside," he said.

But then, when he noticed the homeless man and I were talking, he had a disgusted look on his face.

"Hey drunk beggar, leave him alone," he said to the homeless man.

"Well sir, he's human just like us," Grace snapped back.

I did not realize she was standing behind the court employee.

"That's your wife?" the homeless man asked.

"Yes, that's her," I answered.

"I can tell, she big just like you," he said.

We all started to laugh. As Grace and I were going back in to see the judge, the homeless man shouted,

"Both of you have good hearts, like hearts of doves."

The law had spoken. Xavier was a mere oath removed from legally becoming our son. However, the words of the homeless man continued to ring loudly inside my thoughts. Pain does not lie, he'd said. If my worries had a whisper of truth to them, then his words of wisdom would bear fruit, and our journey would end with wounds. I ran outside to look for the homeless man, but he had left. There was a piece of paper with writing on it on the floor. It was next to where his crutches had been. When I picked up the piece of paper to see what it was, it said: *To Mr. and Mrs. Villard, the hearts of humans plan the course, but God determines their steps (Proverbs 16:9).*

If Salazar and Capricious had not ruined our first court date during our first visit to Haiti, Xavier would have lawfully been our son that day. The adoption would have been sealed. But, Capricious' sister, Marie-Lorraine, who had temporary custody of Xavier was not able to travel. She had been held hostage by a voodoo priest we were told at the last minute. Salazar wanted us to pay for her release, but obviously, Grace and I were never going to allow our hands to be tainted. The wild tale sounded too much like an extortion plot. And so, we had to wait until justice summoned us again to come get our son. Then, Xavier would be forever ours. I began to despise time. It was as though it had become our adversary. We shouldn't allow ourselves to be overpowered by fear, I told Grace. But who was I fooling? After what I had observed during the court proceedings, the thought of losing Xavier swallowed me up with the fierce wind of a powerful storm. On the cusp of relinquishing parental rights of Xavier to us, Salazar looked like a broken man. His eyes were full of tears. His shoulders bowed, way down, revealing his pain. He didn't speak much, aside from answering the judge. "I understand," the judge said to him, comforting Salazar's tears. I was also sobbing on the inside, but it was a father's cry no one could see.

We returned home to spend our last evening with Xavier. We had arranged for Salazar to come back for him later that night.

"Spend as much time as you want with your son," he said.

Although I did not want to, I pleaded with him one last time.

"If you've changed your mind about Xavier, tell me now," I said to him.

Salazar thought it was a silly question.

"Come on, Jude," he answered.

"Why the tears then, Salazar?" I asked.

He laughed, after he had let out a few sneering breaths.

Then, with his voice seemingly bursting with sarcasm,

"He's your son, isn't he?" he said, pointing down to Xavier, who was holding my hand.

"Is he?" I replied with the same scornful thrust, which had cut me within.

Though his scathing remark had stabbed me with a deep wound, I once again heard Xavier's cry. His numbing cries were inside my head.

"Fight for me, Daddy, fight for me," his voice cried a river of tears inside of me.

At that moment, I vowed to continue to fight for my son. I will fight the good fight I said, because of my love for him. But, as we would soon discover, the shrewdness of the hands, which had restored him to life, would stand before us like a beast of the sea, threatening to swallow our love as its prey.

At the house, as soon as the sun started to fall, everyone withdrew into their bedrooms. Grace and I were the only ones left outside with Xavier. Grace thought everyone had gone to bed early to give us time alone with him. We had spent most of the afternoon, and early evening, enjoying our last day with family. And now, the light of day was slowly giving way to nightfall. The fast approaching dark clouds, and ferocious lightning, easily predicted a precipitous downpour. While awaiting Salazar's

I Heard Xavier Cry

return, I sat on the balcony, watching Grace and Xavier cajoling each other. They sat on top of a brick staircase facing the street. It was starting to get dark, but a dim streetlight allowed me a glimpse of their silhouettes. Occasionally, they would move closer to the light, allowing me a better view. Grace had done her best all day to mask her emotions. Yet, the sadness hidden in her heart could not tolerate her silence. The grieving expression on her face betrayed her cover. That look was familiar to me. It had become easily discernable. No matter what Xavier did to get her to smile, her unwavering pose would not surrender. I could hear Xavier's stubborn giggles echoing louder and louder through the gallery. He, too, was sad, but he was trying to make Mommy happy. Grace had been poking him on his huge belly with her fingers, triggering his rush of excitement. But, his struggle in trying to get her to do the same was hopeless. The resilient kid, nonetheless, would not give in so easily. He planted a kiss on her lips and so declared victory. The strong woman's iron posture had been overpowered. Finally, her son had gotten her to smile. At that moment, I turned to the sky and closed my eyes to meditate.

I must have fallen asleep. For when my eyes had opened, Salazar, Grace, and Xavier were all standing in front of me, calling my name. My son was ready to leave me. Without saying a word, Xavier then climbed on top of me. With both hands securely clutching my face, he kissed me on the forehead.

"Daddy, I don't want to go," he cried out, his hands pasted to my face.

He had been at the other end of our signature embrace, every day we had been together. He was now returning the affectionate peck. He firmly held on, grabbing my shoulders and would not let go. I didn't know what to say to him. Perhaps, being abruptly awakened from my sleep was to blame. Everything seemed a blur. Salazar stood in the background, telling Xavier it was time to go. Xavier ignored him. Grace handed Xavier a can of juice, and after he had a sip, he pressed the can against my lips. Then, he carefully sprinkled a few drops in my mouth. Xavier kept looking at me, as he started to cry again. It was the same cry that had been haunting me. I tried to cover my ears with my once rigid heart, but I couldn't. With a massive lump in my throat, I helped myself to some of his juice, hoping it would help conceal my aching heart.

Apparently annoyed that Xavier was not listening to him, and I did not appear to be helping, Salazar raised his voice even louder. Xavier did not turn once to look at him. He kept calling Xavier's name, each time with an angrier tone. Still, his tense words could not detach my son from me. Xavier held on to my shirt with a tighter grip. Tears were flowing down his face, touching his lips.

"Don't want to go, Daddy," he said.

I wiped his tears with a kiss. My son did not want to leave me, and I was not yet ready to let him go. Grace stood idly before us, beholding the quiet storm, while restraining tears. She had always been my tower of strength and voice of dignity. In my weakest hour, she had lifted me up. Hence, she stepped in to cover me once more. She courageously moved to safeguard her husband's integrity. Grace gently took Xavier by the hand and walked him to Salazar. Xavier was pleading with her not to let him go. She kept reassuring him we would be back to bring him home.

"No Mommy, don't let me go," he kept on screaming at the top of his voice.

"We'll come back for you, baby," Grace continued to say to him, as she now had to cradle him in her arms.

By this time, a ferocious rainstorm had begun to come down. A car with an unknown driver had been waiting patiently for Salazar, outside under the thunderous shower. Grace shielded Xavier with her arms and carried him to the car. As Salazar and I followed her outside, my legs shivered in despair with each step. As soon as we had gotten close to the car, the rain began to descend upon us as though it were a coordinated torrent from Heaven. I stood by the car door, downhearted and unable to move. Grace placed Xavier in the backseat. She kissed him on the lips, as though she were smooching her lover. It was a long kiss, a goodbye kiss. She then rubbed her forehead against his.

"I love you," she said to Xavier.

As I was about to send my son away with my own kiss, he reached up and pressed his lips against mine. He then scoured my face with his hands to wipe my tears.

"Come back Daddy, come back," he cried in my ears.

I promised him, I would. And so, in the blink of an eye, our son was gone. My heart sank to the ground when he left. He had disappeared into the storm. We didn't know it then, but it would be our last time seeing Xavier.

SHIFTING ATMOSPHERE

Coming back to Philadelphia, we were downcast. Grace and I slept for almost the entire flight. There wasn't much to talk about. And even if we wanted to vent, we could not gather any strength. Overcome with emotional exhaustion, our mood was subdued. When we finally made it home, my body felt lifeless. It had been the most miserable plane ride we had ever been on. As soon as we walked in the house, Grace went to bed, while I collapsed on the living room sofa. Why did it feel as though my world had ended? We would surely soon go back to get our son, wouldn't we? I thought, with guarded enthusiasm. It felt as though, God had us roaming through a storm we were not yet ready to face. There was a bottle of wine, with a virgin cap, staring at me on the floor. It was the only bottle in the house, a gift from an old friend. Its only purpose had been to serve as a figurine. "Oh God, what a sweet taste of life," I said in my hour of weakness. "Zaire! Zaire!" I cried, before the bottle had put me to sleep against my will.

Was I losing my mind? Even if it were true, I couldn't tell Grace. She would have me committed. After she had nursed me back to health from an undesirable slumber, I told Grace I had been dreaming. But I didn't tell her how much of a horrible nightmare it had been. The homeless man we had met on the steps of the courthouse appeared in my dream. He looked so different. He did not look like someone who had been calling the streets home. And, he was standing on both legs. His clothing, made of fine linen, was a perfect fit as though it had been tailor made. He was traveling with two night birds, one in each hand. Suddenly, one of the night birds flew away and hit a tree. As the man was trying to save it, a car hit him and broke one of his legs. By then, the other night bird had escaped. A peculiar thing then occurred. The night bird who had hit the tree, along with the other one who had escaped, started to chew at the man's flesh. Although I could not tell if he was dead, the man had blood gushing out of his legs. After the night birds had eaten his flesh, and drank his blood, they had suddenly turned into doves. Then, the two doves took off, flying away just as they had done as night birds. They bolted with hastening purpose, as though they wanted to tell the world what had happened to them. But, as they were flying, a rainstorm had ensued, and they both were hit by lightning. Their charred ruins had become a dusky pile of dirt. "Fear not, the time has come," the man then said to me. He was still alive! But then, he started shedding colorful tears. His face turned red, just like his tears. In a fit of anger, he shouted, "My doves, my doves, now their hearts have turned dark." I was then awakened from my sleep.

My soul groaned, yet again, and my heart grew faint. Grace and I were enjoying a beautiful life before this. We were like two birds in a happy nest, sheltered from the troubles of the world. We battled through the pains of life with joy of heart, even after Zaire. But now, it felt as if we were being robbed of our happiness. After a decade, *why now.* Did we need a lesson in love? No one loved more than we did. No one dared to be more selfless. What was the point in arguing with the Lord? There would be no victory in doing such a thing. We had espoused love and made it ruler over our house. But it seemed to want us ripped to shreds. We had traveled across many rivers to answer the cry of an orphan. Were we not doing enough? "Tell me Lord, tell me," I asked, even though I was afraid to speak. It wasn't supposed to be this way. In the castle of love Grace and I had built, I was king, yet now losing my edge.

Shortly after returning from Haiti, the Haitian government underwent a regime change. Haiti had a new charismatic president, who vowed to reestablish law and order. One of his first order of business was to implement drastic changes to the broken Haitian adoption program. The new president did not delay to deliver on a campaign promise. Belizaire warned us about the potential harm the new policy could inflict on our adoption case. The revamped adoption law, he told us, would bring to an end all private adoptions in Haiti, from people living abroad. It certainly was not what we wanted to hear. While the adoption law had not yet been amended, it soon would be. We were racing against time. Our adoption was considered private, so unless we met the deadline imposed, Belizaire avowed, we would have to start all over again. It has been said, that God has a strange sense of humor. Our grim situation wasn't amusing to me. A new policy was necessary, because of the children, they said. They needed to be protected. Thus, the new government applied to be part of the *Hague Convention*. It would help better coordinate international adoption from Haiti, Belizaire told us. Though it would serve Haiti's children well, our adoption of Xavier was in danger of being disrupted because of it.

We had promised Xavier we would be back for him. So what do we do now, I thought? It felt as though so many demonic spirits had conspired to harm us. Yet, I knew even evil spirits were under God's command. That's what the Good Book said. And so, I prayed. "It's in your hands," I said. That same day, my prayer had been answered. Belizaire informed us, all of our documents had been accepted. There was nothing for us to do but wait.

I had prayed to God, and He had answered me. However, fate has an audacious way of sharing its blessings along the path, while remaining stubborn in its track. I had connections inside the *IBESR*; the government agency responsible for overseeing adoptions in Haiti. They were powerful friends, whom I got reacquainted with while we were in Haiti. They had agreed to help with the adoption. But the new regime also brought in a change in leadership within the agency. A new director was appointed, vowing to enforce the newly elected government's commitment in defeating corruption. One of my contacts even got suspended one time for trying to help me. They had already extended so much of themselves, trying to help. I was not going to allow any of them to risk their employment. They were noble men and women. They had gained my utmost gratitude. They also had families to care for. As the new administration needed time to implement Haiti's new adoption policy, there was an additional hurdle to overcome. All adoptions in Haiti were again temporarily suspended. It had happened earlier, right after the earthquake. All international adoptions had been suspended. It was one of the reasons we decided on adopting Xavier through Belizaire. So, yet again, fate had laid its sticky thread before us, like a spider's web. It was determined to have its own ending. Much like death, fate cannot be bribed. Thus, the waiting game we played, trusting in good fortune, while bracing ourselves for jeopardy.

Since Xavier was close to school age, Grace and I had him enrolled in a pre-school program. It was a highly regarded school, Capricious told us. The children were taught in English. It would help Xavier transition much better when he comes home. The school was rather expensive, but worth the cost. We wanted Xavier to have the best education our hands could afford. We were so excited, we quickly sent money for school supplies and uniforms. Our son would be attending a prestigious school. We felt like proud parents. For a while, it made us forget about the wait we had to endure.

I Heard Xavier Cry

"It feels good to be able to send him to school," I told Grace. "I love him."

Underneath the shadow of that love, however, laid a mountain of mistrust. Therefore, I had my cousin Mario inspect the school. The reviews were beyond belief. "Crème de la crème," he said. I knew it was nothing more than an over-glorified daycare. But we didn't care. If it was the "cream of the crop" Mario suggested it to be, our son would then be esteemed amongst the best. Xavier would be rubbing shoulders with sons and daughters of Haiti's rich and famous. The pre-kindergarten program was well known for its stylish campus, and artistry in teaching children, Mario told us. We had to once more increase Xavier's monthly allowance, as the school required additional funds for extracurricular activities. There were other schools nearby, Capricious admitted that were not as costly. We wanted the little orphan boy to stand tall.

As we impatiently waited, day after day, and weeks after weeks, for the suspension of all adoptions to be lifted, our patience started to wear thin. Since Salazar was still Xavier's legal guardian, we had him apply to get a passport for Xavier. We had waited long enough. Perhaps it was because of those horrifying thoughts, which kept me awake at night. They refused to go away. They were pressing me to hurry. Salazar and

Capricious were acting even more peculiar, ever since Grace and I returned from Haiti. Xavier, Capricious complained, only wanted to wear the clothes he wore while with us in Jacmel. We told her it might have been because he missed being with us. It seemed to bother her a whole lot, as the words hurled out of her mouth with utter disgust. Salazar's strange behavior was turning ever more into a father's scorn. He began to boast about how much time and money he and Capricious had invested in Xavier. "You have done great things for Xavier," he said, "but we've done just as much." Grace thought he had been harboring jealousy in his heart. It was a cry to run away, but we couldn't. We loved Xavier too much.

If Xavier were allowed to visit us, our minds would then be at peace. It was the reason why we rushed to get him a passport. We wanted to be with our son. When he was happy, we were happy. And if he didn't feel well, we carried his sickness with us. One time, he was stricken with thyroid fever and had to be in the hospital for nearly two weeks. Grace and I felt so helpless. We wanted to be the ones to care for our son. Grace was ready to get on the next flight to Haiti, but the doctor said Xavier would get well. Capricious assured us she would nurse him back to health. A few days later, she sent us a picture of our baby boy. He looked happy to Grace, but I saw sadness on his face.

I Heard Xavier Cry

His eyes were speaking to me. They were telling me *when,* Daddy, *when.*

DIVIDED LOYALTY

While at work one evening, the much-anticipated phone call came. Although it was not the one we were anxiously waiting for, it was good news. It had me hunkered down in my seat in torment, however. Capricious had delivered a baby boy. She bore a son, who was flesh of her flesh. I had been struggling with these awful thoughts, but there were more of them now in my head. How was it going to affect my son? Capricious loved Xavier as her own, but with the reawakening of a barren womb, would her affection for him be the same. She wanted so much to have her own child, not even Xavier could bring comfort to her once aching womb. Yet, our love for him had brought comfort to ours. Though Capricious had raised Xavier almost from birth, he was not like a son to her, as she had so passionately professed. If he were, I thought, we would not have been the ones struggling with the law for his love. I knew it was unfair for me to think that way. She had every right to want her own child. Now that God had loosened her womb, would her love for her newborn royal son bring sorrow to the heart of our adopted prince.

Fear had unleashed its grit like a warmonger. When it couldn't stifle our love, it wanted to choke us to death. A volcanic wave suddenly erupted with the birth of the new baby. Expecting Capricious to care for the two young princes under her wings without favor would have been too much to ask. At the very least, we did not want Xavier to feel neglected. Our fear had become more than frightening thoughts. There were many nights when talking to my son, I could hear the lonely cries stringing from his voice. Xavier was soon about to turn two. He was better at expressing his pain. "Home, Daddy," he would whisper in an almost muted sadness. His dad had heard his cry. It felt as though I was choking in my own rage and tears. Xavier was my son, but he was Grace's *baby*.

"Xavier's miserable, he's sad," I would complain to Grace,

"Of course he is," she would chime in with the ire of a distraught mother.

When asked why Xavier sounded so unhappy, Capricious said it was because her new baby made him jealous. One night, Xavier sat on the floor crying for hours she said, as he watched the couple and their newborn prince crowded together in a picturesque family bond. Without a doubt, my son was caged in by loneliness in his own home. It was no longer his home, I said to Grace. His home was with us, and he knew it.

Though the couple had restored hope in him, Xavier had taken a back seat to their inheritance. In our home, he would have a crown above his head. My son was being treated like a black sheep. "The little boy"—that's how Capricious began to refer to him; the one she once called her son. She began to chastise Xavier with vile words, which cut so deep, she might as well had thrown stones at him.

"You're starting to irritate me; you act like an idiot," she growled at Xavier one night.

"He's changed, Jude. I don't know what's wrong with him, but he's changed," Capricious complained, referring to Xavier. "He just sits there like a dummy and refuses to speak."

My heart began to race, faster and faster, high pulse, low pulse, angry, and sad. I had enough anger within to send me to Hell. Things needed to change.

I Heard Xavier Cry

In a desperate effort to free Xavier from Capriccios' wrath, we decided it was finally time for our son to move in with family. Grace's aunt agreed to take him in. But it wouldn't be for another three to four weeks. She was away, caring for her sick husband, who worked and lived in a distant province. We didn't mind the wait, since it would only be a couple of weeks. Meanwhile, it became a struggle, trying to make sense of the couple's outlandish behavior. Soon after telling Capricious we would be moving Xavier, Salazar told us Xavier's passport had gone missing. Was this a joke? I thought. Not even a full week had passed since Salazar had picked it up at the agency. He had no idea how it got lost. The rain barrel of deceit started to crack. Capricious then began to tell a different story. One of Salazar's relatives, she said, had by mistake taken the passport with him to the Dominican Republic. That family member had somehow misplaced the passport. We had to send money to get another one done. Capricious quickly came to her husband's defense, after I told her their stories didn't add up. She claimed she had not yet told Salazar how the passport had suddenly disappeared. They were like rain barrels, Capricious and her husband, like a rain barrel whose thirst is never satisfied. When I told Capricious how upset we had been because of the missing passport, it made her gasped with sarcasm. "Well, I'm sorry, but a passport is not a million bucks," she said. To her, the reward of our hard labor had come from the dewy sky. There would be more ambiguous tales, hails of unforeseen exploits. Nothing made sense. The dark cloud of mystery was about to reach its apex.

Close to a week after telling Capricious, Xavier would be moving with Grace's aunt, the pulse of our adoption journey had shifted gear. Although Capricious yielded quickly to our demand, I wondered how she was going to react when it was time for Xavier to leave. "Where your treasure is, *there* your heart will be," the Good Book said. While her heart no longer danced to the same rhythm for Xavier, I started to think, she still looked at him as a prized jewel. The capricious woman was always one step ahead. Before I could even get a chance to reflect on everything that had befallen us, she bolted out of town with the haste of a restless bandit. Salazar, she told us, suffered a nearly fatal car accident in the Dominican Republic. He was unable to move or speak. Though she did not know for sure, Capricious was told Salazar was probably in a coma. She needed to leave immediately, she said; so she could be with her husband. Her newborn son, along with Xavier, were left with her sister Marie-Loraine. The young woman apparently had to interrupt her studies. There was no one else to look after the children. Since we did not know when Capricious would return, we wired additional funds to her. While she was gone, we wanted to make sure Xavier would have everything he needed. About a week after Capricious left, Marie-Loraine was calling. She needed money, because Xavier had nothing to eat. There had to be some sort of misunderstanding. When asked if she had heard from Capricious, Marie-Lorraine said she hadn't heard from her since Capricious left. She was still waiting for Capricious to call.

When Capricious left, she didn't leave a number to contact her. She had promised to call as soon as she arrived in Santo Domingo. But, nearly a week had gone by, we were still waiting for her to call. With Marie-Lorraine not being able to get in touch with her sister, I began to worry. Why would she leave a newborn child behind for so long without calling? Something awful must have happened. Perhaps, Salazar's condition was worse than she thought. Then, nearly two weeks after not having heard from Capricious, Salazar called. Thank God! I thought. He must have recovered from the terrible accident. He sounded pretty aloof when I started to ask about the accident. Then again, this was how he'd always been. He was always evasive and standoffish. He often acted as though he and his wife were being put on trial. Salazar did not disclose what had happened to him. This was awkward, much like what a dream should be. It wasn't. Salazar was not even willing to tell me whether or not he had been in a coma.

"So, why is it you're calling me?" I asked, before inquiring about Capricious.

He was calling because he needed money.

"You're kidding me, right?" I said to him.

He sounded so much like a man in distress. I couldn't bear to tell him no. In spite of our differences, Salazar had helped us a great deal with the adoption, especially at the beginning. He would say to me, "Now, you will have a son. Xavier will be your heir." Safeguarding my legacy by adopting a child, did not matter as much I told him, as cementing a legacy of love. I, nonetheless, appreciated his thoughtful words. At the time, he, just like me, was a married man who had not yet experienced the joy of fatherhood. It could have been his way of showing sympathy. Even so, things had changed. His duplicitous schemes and sneering remarks while in Haiti had turned him into an adversary. Perhaps it was fate, justifying our generosity till the bittersweet end. We sent the money without any ill will. When I finally inquired about Capricious, there was suddenly an eerie silence on the phone. "She's not around," Salazar mumbled, after his conspicuous delay. He was speaking in such a dim voice, I could barely hear him. It was as if he had been nervously following his wife's command. I knew she was there. I heard her capricious whispers. While she may have thought her muffled deceit was completely veiled, I heard her faint voice in the background. As cunning as a fox, she was carefully guiding her husband's words. I felt no need to berate her shameless ploy. There wasn't a trace of doubt left in my mind, she had astutely plotted her gambit, as in a game of chess, using Xavier as pawn.

Grace and I did not join in the fight to save the orphans as willing victims. We were not going to surrender our souls as martyrs of love. "We cannot allow ourselves to be played like fools," Grace said to me. She uttered the words with a remorseful anger. We joined hands with the couple to help conquer a good cause. At least, that's what we thought. But, we were being led like sheep. There had been times when we wanted to turn our backs and walk away. We couldn't, as we then started to feel the weight of guilt. Leaving Xavier behind would be like walking away from love. He was in need of our love, just as much as we desperately wanted to love him. The Spirit then started speaking to us in our dreams. It always carried peace with it. But, underneath its wings laid its zeal. It was a fighting Spirit. "Fight until the last cry," the Spirit would say to me, portending what was to come. It had been weeping, singing to me in my dreams since Capricious left. I was never able to understand the lyrics of its sad songs. One morning, in a vision, as I wasn't sure if I was fully awake or still asleep. The words of the Spirit had become clear to me. It would be its last song before the end of our journey.

I could hear the faded voices emitting from the television in the room. Unable to move, I saw a pageantry of angels standing before me. They were singing to me, as though my eyes were now "opened." Dressed all in white, they started flinging fire out of their mouths every time the chorus paused. It frightened me so much, I wanted to close my eyes, but I couldn't. Then, I saw my lifeless body lying in a coffin, being launched upright by a brisk wind into a stealth, maroon sky. A comforting light all of a sudden appeared. It encircled the dim coffin. Both hands nervously clenching, the rest of my body was still frozen. The loud and sudden thumping of my heartbeat increasingly hammered my chest. In a flash, Salazar and Capricious appeared. They were both sitting on top of my bedroom ceiling. Clouds of dust, rapidly formed through the cracks. The ceiling began to crumble. "Move away from there!" I shouted. Capricious, dressed in a black, priestly robe, seemingly scowling in defeat, stared me down with tears of fire in her eyes. She then threw me a set of keys.

I Heard Xavier Cry

"Here are your damn house keys," she cried, with flames of fire coming out of her mouth.

"I don't want them anymore," Capricious shouted with resounding thunder in her voice.

The phone then started ringing, awaken me from the nightmarish sleep. It was Capricious on the line, searing with rage. She started to attack me with a barrage of vindictive insults. Her angry words, filled with so much hatred, one would have thought I was a monster.

"You're a tyrant, an evil man, and a horrible father," she bellowed.

Finally, the narrowing umbilical string of our attachment to Xavier had been severed.

"You will never see Xavier as long as I live," Capricious declared. "I hate you," she said.

I listened to her audacious bombast without uttering a word.

"As of today," she said, "Forget about me and erase Xavier from your memory."

Those were Capricious' last words to me. The oracle, at last, had come to an end

MISSION DEFEATED

After we had sent Salazar the money he needed, we did not hear from the couple for nearly a year. They appeared to have vanished without a trace. No one could find them. Not even Niko had heard from them. We had also lost contact with Capricious' sister, Marie-Loraine. Her number had been disconnected. We spent months, after months, trying to figure out what had happened to our son, to no end. Our only source of connection with him was through Capricious' sister. With her phone being out of service, we had lost hope. We had not spoken to her since the day after Salazar and I last talked. Salazar claimed he was still in the hospital that day. He didn't have a number for us to reach him. It was my last time hearing from the couple.

And thus, in an instant, panic had taken over. We didn't know where our son was. Our whole world appeared to be crumbling. All we had hoped for was to love, when we answered the cry of the orphan. Though his cries had become louder, we couldn't hear him. Grace started to disconnect. Her resilient heart could no longer bear the burden of holding on to a broken dream. One breath at a time, the vision started to fade away. We could no longer ignore the facts. We were at a crossroad, unsure where the journey would lead us.

Almost a week to a year after the couple had disappeared, we finally received a call from Capricious. She told an outrageous tale, which nearly made Grace and I choked in disgust. She and her husband had been hiding in fear of a voodoo priestess, she said, who had been tormenting them. The woman was no stranger to them, Capricious told us. It was Salazar's own sister. She had been attempting to harm them. So they ran away, both her and her husband, fleeing to the Dominican Republic for refuge.

"I'm so sorry about everything," Capricious atoned.

I could hear the tears being wiped from her face. Unable to drum up the right words to express my anger, I listened with an angry silence. I did not want to spoil her remorseful speech.

"Please, I beg of you, say something?" Capricious pleaded.

The fading cry of my son sprung again inside my head.

"Where is Xavier?' I asked.

She wavered endlessly, as though she were humming to a melody, before finally admitting he was still with her sister in Haiti.

"Is your son with you?" I then curiously inquired, compelling her to answer what I had already suspected.

"Yes, he's with me," her voice shaky.

They were still in the Dominican Republic. Salazar had gone back to Haiti, she said, to pick up their son, but couldn't bring Xavier back with him. His passport was not yet ready. Salazar was afraid to cross the border with him.

"It would have been too risky," Capricious asserted. "We were going to go back for him," she contended.

I couldn't believe what I was hearing. There is no way to explain what happened next. As I was scolding her, while still trying to hold on to my dignity,

I Heard Xavier Cry

Capricious stopped me dead in my track. She stopped me from speaking that is.

"You're such a good man, be kind to me," she said.

She, once again, started to cry.

"Please, Jude, please forgive me," Capricious sobbed, arousing my spirit of sympathy. "There's a lot you don't know. Trust me, just trust me," she said.

Why was she calling me *now*? *There* was the simmering charm of the unpredictable femme fatale. She knew where I had been weak, so she pounced. Ensnaring me into her web of deceit, as if I was her prey. She needed money to travel to Haiti so she could gather all of Xavier's belongings. She and her sister, Marie-Loraine, would then travel by bus with Xavier to Port-au-Prince.

"Xavier needs to be with his new family," she said.

Capricious had finally decided it was time for her to bring Xavier to Grace's aunt. Since she was still afraid to return home because of Salazar's sister, she and Marie-Lorraine were going to meet at a friend's house. Besides, she needed to give Marie-Lorraine her keys, she said. Xavier's birth certificate, along with other important documents were in a locked bedroom at the house. God! Finally, my son would be where he belongs.

By this time, so much had changed. Our attorney still held hope. The courts had ruled favorably on our behalf. One more trip, Xavier would then officially be ours. One more trip, and Heaven would rejoice with us. We called Belizaire immediately. "Let the judge know we're ready," I said to him. We were getting ready to pack our bags to go claim our son. He laughed, Belizaire did, when we told him what had happened. His laughter tasted sour. "Congratulations my friend," he said, with a hearty laugh. It sounded more like a wound from a friend. How else could I explain it? His words of praise had entered my mind with trepidation.

The day Capricious arrived in Haiti to bid farewell to Xavier, the sun didn't shine so bright. The sky had opened up, letting down the dew of heaven. Only this time, it felt as though Heaven had been mourning. "Wow, it's raining cats and dogs today," I remember Grace saying. It reminded us of the last time we saw Xavier. However, it was going to be a different day. It would be the day, when the son whom we thought had been lost in the storm, had lastly found his way back into our hearts. Though we rejoiced loudly, the sun would not show its face. It was odd, that such a blessed day could look and feel like the same day I had shed fearful buckets of tears for my son.

I Heard Xavier Cry

Suddenly, my phone was ringing. Although it was an unknown number, I was afraid to answer.

"Pick up the damn phone," Grace spewed out. "What if it's Capricious for God sake?"

And it was. Capricious was calling with the most dreaded telephone call no parent wants to hear. Xavier had broken both of his legs while jumping out of a balcony.

"Oh my God!" I shouted, clutching my head with both hands. "How could this have happened?"

This was my first time hearing my son's voice, in what seemed like an eternity. We did not know what to expect. Speaking to him that day, he remembered who we were.

"Xavier, its Daddy. Do you remember me?" I nervously asked.

It took him some time to answer. However, he recalled who we were.

"Daddy! You come back?" he screamed with a mouthful of cheer.

But then, he started to cry a little, as though it were a bitter cry for help. When asked if he was in any pain, his voice dimmed even more. How awful, I thought. His birthday was only a couple of days away. Still, we were so thankful our son would soon be with us. Even though we had sent money for Capricious to take him to the hospital, he was still at home when we spoke with him. We had spent so many hours trying to reach Capricious before she had finally answered. She could not fully explain why Xavier had not yet gone to the hospital. They were waiting for a driver, she said, who had been delayed. There weren't any ambulances to call from their remote location, Capricious said. This was a few hours after my son had broken his legs. While Xavier wasn't screaming in pain, Grace and I were anxious. Capricious acted as if she had no sympathy for our grief.

"This is not the U.S., okay. Here, we wait," She said, when we told her how upset we were.

By nightfall, Xavier had returned home from the hospital with both legs in a cast, Capricious told us. Perhaps, she felt trapped in her own cage. She offered to send us pictures of Xavier's broken legs. Days went by, without us receiving any photos. "A technical malfunction," Capricious concluded might have caused the delay. She had posted the pictures on the internet, she said. When asked if she would be able to send them via attachment to a text message, or email, as she and Salazar had done in the past, the volatile temptress imploded.

"I knew it! You don't trust me anymore," she said.

Her sly remark went unanswered. The moment of truth was finally upon us.

"It's time for Xavier to go," I told Capricious, reminding her, she had promised to take him to Grace's aunt.

"No, Jude, please let me take him back with me," she said.

"Back where?" The words screeching out of my mouth.

My throat was beginning to feel sore. Capricious wanted to take Xavier to the Dominican Republic for him to get medical care.

"Let him go, Capricious," I said to her.

"But they have good doctors there. He needs to go with me," She answered.

Her voice then drifted behind the shadow of her tears. The more I struggled with her, the harder she fought. Even my fervent appeal to have Xavier receive care at home with us was met with contempt.

"Capricious, my dear," I pleaded with her. "You've even rejected our request to apply for an emergency visa."

She ignored my plea, as though my words were rootless.

Who could blame her? I had incessantly allowed her to parade triumphantly in front of me to the sounds of tambourines, while I watched helplessly as a spectator. Because of my love for Xavier, my endless love for my son, my discerning wall had crumbled. A dishonest heart had decided to ruin mine. Her brazen display of confidence, however, was about to meet its end.

At sunrise the following day, Capricious, yet again, attempted to lure me into her serpentine web. This time, she was even more audacious. She called, asking for money so she could take Xavier to Santo Domingo.

"Xavier either stays with our family or," not even allowing me to finish.

"Or what?" she sighed with the sneer of a predator. "You won't do it.," she said.

She began to scream with a rebellious fury.

"You love him too much," Capricious hollered, testing my will.

That same evening, as nightfall drew near, the weary pulse of a father's love was about to be put to the test. At first, the carefully crafted texts were nothing more than petty rants from a scornful woman.

But then, as the night wore on, their tone began to sting like a venomous bite of a viper.

"You are a despicable man, evil, and heartless," Capricious wrote.

"What kind of a father are you?"

She continued to insult me. She had even threatened to report us to the police. *"I will tell them, you guys are baby snatchers."* The woman had apparently gone insane. One minute she was insulting me, then suddenly, her dreadful jeers had turned into admiration.

"I know you're a good dad," she texted, praising me.

"I know you love your son."

The texts kept rolling through my phone. They looked like closing credits on a screen projector. I couldn't tell whether it was a frantic struggle to manipulate me or the shifty mood of a schizophrenic outburst. As I was leaving work to go home, her chilling vitriol resumed. I walked in the door after arriving home and showed Grace my phone. She stared at it for a long time, pasting the screen with her thumb without saying a word. She then let out a deep breath. The phone was once again buzzing. Grace handed it back to me. "Baby, it's over," she whispered in an almost uncaring voice. My lovely Grace had lost her will to fight.

As we were now ignoring her messages, Capricious began to swamp my phone with calls. The never-ending thudding of my muted phone went on all night until dawn, vibrating what seemed like every second of the night. Grace, petrified and unable to sleep, finally turned my phone off. By then, the light of day had already come. As Grace was heading to work, I turned my phone on. There were over a dozen voice messages, twenty missed calls, and more than one hundred text messages. They were all from Capricious. After listening to her messages, my heart began to sob with pity.

"Jude, I'm on the bus. I am leaving without Xavier." Another—"That's it, Jude. You left me without a choice, I'm abandoning your son."

A few minutes later, my phone again was buzzing with a voice message alert. It was Capricious again.

"I couldn't leave; I came back to get Xavier, okay?" she wailed endlessly.

It seemed as though she had been awake all night. Her bizarre night-time antic reminded me of what many in Haiti reckoned as folk tales of—Loups Garou (sorcerers with wings). It frightened Grace so much, she didn't think it was funny when I joked about Capricious acting like a vampire. I also should have been terrified by her midnight madness. She had led me to believe she was a church woman, but she had kept her evil deeds hidden behind a mask.

That morning, Grace must have had her own divine intuition. She awoke from the gory night with a strange request. "Ask to speak with Salazar," Grace suggested, before leaving for work. It seemed rather foolish, I thought. Both Capricious and her husband were one and the same. When Capricious called that morning, still relentless in her quest for money, I asked to speak with Salazar.

"Tell your husband to call me," I said to her.

Although she had heard me, there was a long, eerie pause before she again continued her crusade for money. In a last desperate appeal, my tone wary, as I did not know what this woman who sounded so irrational would do to my son, I once again pleaded to speak with Salazar.

"Can I have his number," I asked.

All I remember hearing then was the stillness of the dial. The silence would linger until the next morning, the morning of my vision. Then, the cherubs' hymns had become clear as the light of day. There was something in what Grace pushed me to ask that must have troubled Capricious' soul. The hearts destined to love Xavier had been pierced with a wisdom arrow, with these last words, "As of today, forget about me, erase Xavier from your memory."

FILLING UP
THE AWKWARD SPACES

The long train ride must have been exhausting. It was now a quarter past midnight. The love of my life had finally made it home. I could hear his steps, even before he had entered the room. His pace was slow and gentle, as though he were strolling to a night waltz. He then stood above me, gently running his fingers through my hair. "I love you," he whispered in my ear, after planting a warm kiss on my cheek. To him, it may have looked like I was sound asleep, but I wasn't. This was how we greeted each other every working night for the past ten years. Yet, this night, he didn't lie down next to me like he usually does, stroking my back until I fall asleep. He sat at the edge of the bed, staring blindly at the television screen.

"Jude?"

He seemed lost in his own world. As I got up to get closer to him, I could hear the frustration in his voice.

"We're too damn good to people," he said, turning to me with a snickering grin.

It wasn't an honest smile. Not the one that always tickles my heart like a butterfly. Laughter had always gotten us through, out of the blues, that is.

It had been over a decade since I fell in love with this man. He had never ceased to love me back. "That's why I love you," I would often say to tease him. The man that I love had been wounded. Though he had always been a caring man, he saw too much of himself in people. The reflection in the mirror had not been so kind. For when light reflects upon darkness, even the dark appears bright. We had been deceived. Losing Xavier had crushed both our spirits. But to Jude, our short-lived eureka moment had revealed a greater sin. Surely, God had not forsaken us, in answering the cry of an orphan. And so, why such a long journey? Was there a lesson to be learned?

I Heard Xavier Cry

Nearly two years had passed, but the scars remained. While there were many pictures to gratify the eye, the indelible memories had been recorded in our hearts. The ocean swims right before nightfall, our promenades through some of the lush places in Jacmel, and Xavier's charming smile, all delighted the heart. Memories often lie they say, but not ours, not when it comes to Xavier. The locust of greed had taken our son away, but not our love for him. There had been many grieving nights, but not without guilt. How could we? But we did. The suffocating noose slowly stealing our breath needed to be cut off. I thought perhaps, Salazar could have helped, but he as well seemed to be spellbound by his wife's magic charm. We still kept in touch with one of Xavier's uncles. Big Manno, as Jude likes to call him, met with us briefly while we were in Haiti. When we were trying to adopt Xavier, the judge had asked if he had any other relatives. This was how we had come to know him. He lived in a distant province and wasn't much involved in Xavier's life. He was struggling to take care of a wife and four young children. Jude had tried for so long to get in touch with him after the ordeal. We were curious to find out how Xavier was doing. When we finally spoke with Manno, several months later, he told us he had heard about the horrible affair. He thought it was a well-planned scheme for money. "Both you and your wife are a little naïve," he said. Talking to him, helped in relieving some of the guilt we still felt. It was exactly what we needed to put an end to that chapter of our lives. The wings of the journey had been buried beyond resuscitation.

It is just as Aunt Clara had taught us, "Love is not always comfortable," she said, "but you have to give it your best." Aunt Clara knew how to love. Nevertheless, *hurt* also found its niche in her bosom. That's why she was here—you know—in the U.S. Aunt Clara had helped restore so many lives. But she had to run. She fled like a dove. Some, wanted to harm her because of her good works. "One can never see the evil hidden in the hearts of people." She would often say to us. We had come to understand that evil ourselves.

Though it would take a flood of deceits, and a broken heart, Jude and I finally understood the angels' chorus. The ones in our dreams. Their words of wisdom had also come to me. In a dream the night before Capricious stole our joy, I saw Salazar tied to a fig tree. Both of his hands were shackled behind him. He was struggling to escape, but he couldn't. Then, from nowhere, my husband suddenly appeared. He was standing near the same fig tree. I looked again, closely at my husband and saw three giant locusts climbing on his back. Their weight was too much for him to bear. He was struggling to get rid of them. Though they wanted to overpower him, he didn't utter a word. As he was falling to the ground, the locusts still crawling on his back, I ran to his rescue. Then, the cherubim suddenly appeared. They had gotten to him before I did. They grabbed all three swarming hoppers with their bare hands and started to sing a curious song. Everything then started making sense. At the time Jude and I were trying to adopt Xavier, our compassionate hearts had fallen prey to many deceits. We rejoiced with those who were joyful and wept with those in grief. Yet, sour exploits still rested at our door. Though we had not inspired their loathing feast, nor reserved a seat at their table of reproach, we were forced to taste their bitter betrayal. "He's evil," they said, condemning Jude when they could no longer eat from the fruit of his kind heart. However, he had, we had both gone above and beyond all secret things. Surely, all good deeds, and all hidden things belong to God, don't they

?

I knew what was troubling my husband the night he came home from work in distress. What the angels sang to him, they had sung to me as well.

"I am sending you out like sheep among wolves; therefore, be as shrewd as snakes and as innocent as doves." (Mathew 10:16)

TO XAVIER,

Son, wherever you are, we loved you. We love you still and always will. We tried so desperately to hold on to you. But true destiny took you out of our hands. We pray for you every day. We pray that God leads your paths. God has many soldiers, and we know that He will choose one who will finish what we started. We have gained so much wisdom because of you. In the short time we got to spend together, you brought us so much joy. It has greatly impacted our lives. We pray that you will forgive the hands who refused to give you away. And, forgive us, for giving up and lacking the courage to continue to fight for you. You may not have known your birth parents, yet we are certain they loved you even more than we ever will. Son, there is nothing about you not to love. You will always be in our hearts. So, rise and shine until we meet again, on earth or in Heaven.

ALSO BY JUDE EMMANUEL

Violin
Son of an Abuser

God, Love, Country
Shouldn't We All Fall in Love?

www.ingramcontent.com/pod-product-compliance
Lightning Source LLC
Chambersburg PA
CBHW061643040426
42446CB00010B/1549